SAMUEL L. CHELL

The Dynamic Self: Browning's Poetry of Duration

ELS
EDITIONS

© 1984 by Samuel L. Chell

ELS Editions
Department of English
University of Victoria
Victoria, BC
Canada V8W 3W1
www.elseditions.com

Founding Editor: Samuel L. Macey

General Editor: Luke Carson

Printed by CreateSpace

English literary studies monograph series
ISSN 0829-7681 ; 32
ISBN-10 0-920604-17-X
ISBN-13 978-0-920604-17-5

CONTENTS

PREFACE

Acknowledgements not only tend to sound promotional in thanking numerous eminent readers of the manuscript but often require the writer to double back on himself in order to absolve his readers of responsibility for defects remaining in the final draft. The speaker of "By the Fireside" discovers that "a soul declares itself — to wit, / By its fruit, the thing it does!" My gratitude is especially extended to those who have not tasted the fruit but without whom there would have been none to harvest. It was Zilpha Colee who first planted the seed, Donald Smalley who nurtured it, Todd K. Bender who brought it to fruition, and Charlotte Chell who convinced me that judicious pruning would yield the most palatable result.

More immediately, thanks are due the National Endowment for the Humanities and the Midwest Faculty Seminar of the University of Chicago for assistance that enabled me to purchase time when it was most needed. In typing the manuscript, Gladys Dart generously gave of her time when there appeared none to give. My father, to whose memory these pages are dedicated, taught me time's true worth.

SAMUEL L. CHELL

INTRODUCTION

The designation "poet-philosopher," once reverently bestowed upon Browning, encouraged a merciless dissection of the poet following his death. Henry Jones, in *Browning as Philosopher and Religious Teacher*,[1] discredited Browning's competence as a thinker by accusing him of denying all knowledge and appealing solely to the emotions. But it was Santayana's indictment of Browning as a barbarian poet[2] that drew up the major battle lines. Finding Browning deficient in artistic detachment and aesthetic form, Santayana charged the poet with morbid self-consciousness and an irrational soul incapable of giving itself over to permanent objects.

T. S. Eliot and the new critics took the bait, either dismissing Browning outright or reading as isolated artifacts a severely limited number of the poems. During the reassessment of Browning that began in the 1950's and carried into the 1960's some critics applauded the poet for his gusto or primitivism[3] while others sought to preserve his philosophical integrity.[4] Important studies by Robert Langbaum and J. Hillis Miller[5] rescued Browning's work from anachronism by affording it a central place within the romantic tradition, redefined as a vital stream of experience extending from the nineteenth century into our own times. In the 1970's the primacy of this tradition and of Browning's place within it were vigorously argued by Harold Bloom in an impressive series of works.[6] A consequence of this rejuvenated interest in the romantic tradition of poetry has been a sharper focus on the informing spirit behind and within the poem. The critical endeavor to draw that animating principle out of the poem has, in turn, led to an inevitable concern with the poet's understanding of time.

As studies by George Mead and Georges Poulet make clear,[7] time for the romantic is a process inseparable from the notion of self. Especially crucial to the romantic's quest for identity is the effort to recapture the past as a significant element in present experience. Without duration, without a principle of continuity of past with present, it becomes meaningless to speak of "self." It was not until Kant that the individual could claim from modern philosophy such a unifying principle in the response to temporal flow. Humean empiricism, by regarding the self as a mechanical association of impressions and reducing all knowledge to a sensory basis, tended to deprive the individual of personal identity.[8] By the nineteenth century, however, a new subjective time-consciousness enabled the individual to come to a full realization of the critical importance of time in human life, forced the individual to take time "seriously." This preoccupation, as Jerome Buckley has shown in *The Triumph of Time*,[9] was never more conspicuous than among poets and novelists of the Victorian era.

Of all Victorian authors, none is better qualified for a time-centered study than Robert Browning. Browning's re-creation of the dramatic past and hearty acceptance of the present are celebrated aspects of his poetry, as are his view of life as endless progress and his quest for "the infinite moment." Certainly some consideration of the role of time is indispensable to any appraisal of Browning's poetry and its place in the modern tradition. The pervasive and deep influence of time upon Browning's poetry has, in fact, been long recognized. F. R. G. Duckworth, in *Browning: Background and Conflict*, found deep-seated conflict in the mind and art of the poet — a conflict directly produced by the problem of time. Because Browning tried to present two opposite points of view — reality as timeless (the infinite moment) versus reality as an endless series of time (the doctrine of the imperfect) — his life and poetry, in Duckworth's estimation, suffered much disorder. In a more recent essay, " 'Eternity Our Due': Time in the Poetry of Robert Browning,"[11] J. W. Harper reaffirms that the principal concern in Browning's poetry is the problem of time. Echoing Duckworth's earlier position, Harper finds Browning trapped between the irreconcilable views of timelessness and unending time.

William Whitla's *The Central Truth: The Incarnation in Browning's Poetry*[12] is in large part a response to the critics who find disunity and confusion in Browning's treatment of time. The conflict between temporal existence and the desire for an "infinite moment" is indeed the central thematic problem of all of Browning's poetry, according to Whitla, but Browning is consistently able to solve the problem through an incarnational experience. Valuable as Whitla's study is in underscoring Browning's artistic unity (the monologues are systematically classified according to a trinitarian pattern) and in reemphasizing Browning's Christian inheritance, its thesis finally seems overstated. The Incarnation becomes a sort of *deus ex machina* so that Browning may never fail in his role as problem solver. Time, in turn, is abstracted into a theological problem. Its dynamic effect upon personality and inseparability from a sense of self, its psychological reality within a subject ever conscious of its passing — these primary temporal concerns can not be adequately accounted for by reliance on primitive Christian theology alone.

Herbert Tucker's recent study, *Browning's Beginnings*, partly redresses Whitla's focus by examining the aesthetic implications of Browning's innate love of the future. In penetrating, rigorous analyses of Browning's early poetry, Tucker sees Browning's attitude of anticipation as a correlative to his art of disclosure. The poet's fear of completion corresponds, in turn, to the anticlosural tendency of his poems, which can be viewed as self-defenses against "the threat that there may be nothing left to say."[13] An eloquent and important contribution to Browning criticism, Tucker's study nevertheless tends to sacrifice the past and present to the future, presenting a poet whose constant beginnings must call into question the possibility of purposeful becoming.[14]

Browning's interest in the possibility of genuine self-realization is the problem addressed in two recently published studies, Constance W. Hassett's *The Elusive Self in the Poetry of Robert Browning*[15] and E. Warwick Slinn's *Browning and the Fictions of Identity*.[16] Insisting on the impulse toward self-assessment as the fundamental issue in Browning's art, Hassett sees honest and full confession as crucial to a speaker's conversion, or moral regeneration. Seemingly problematic is her insistence that Browning's characters are all motivated to speak by the imperative need to know themselves, even if the impulse toward self-knowledge is frequently obstructed by attendant anxieties. Slinn's argument provides a balance to this emphasis on the confessional nature of Browning's monologues. Slinn sees Browning's speakers as verbal actors who seize upon artifice to maintain the illusion of personal identity. Whereas for Hassett, Browning's characters fail to change, for Slinn they succeed in not changing. They reinforce false conceptualizations of themselves by assuming a continuity between experience and reality in contrast to Browning who, according to Slinn, questions the truth of experience. The poet who finally emerges in this reading is a confirmed skeptic, constantly undermining human claims to truth through a multiplicity of subverting ironies.

The present study combines Tucker's emphasis on temporal concerns with Hassett's and Slinn's investigation of the role of self in Browning's poetry. Reflecting much late nineteenth century thought, Browning regarded time neither as an abstraction nor as a threat but as the dynamic, creative medium in which the individual expresses and discovers a continuous self. Browning's psychological drama looks forward to the internal, subjective novel, in which dramatic action is located within the consciousness of heroes frequently estranged from their worlds. Unlike the "free association" of thoughts characteristic of the stream-of-consciousness novel, however, Browning's monologues contain rhetorical strategies that continually bring the

9

problem of time to the surface. Just as time in his poetry is a conscious concern demanding a right response, time in this study will primarily refer to the universal problem of change and its relation to the concept of self, the formal aspects of temporal experience emerging from this basic thematic concern. Functioning in the monologues as a test of character, time provides a touchstone to the poetry — to structure and meaning as well as to the aesthetic response produced by their fusion.

I have focussed on Browning's understanding of time as duration because it not only facilitates entrance to individual poems but clarifies Browning's poetic development and finally comes closest to an unmasking of the poet's creative self. That self, which the poet would describe as "ever a fighter," is best understood when it is enacted by the language of the poem rather than advanced by an overly busy ringside commentator. Although Browning often speaks out explicitly on the relationship between temporal process and spiritual growth in the poems following *The Ring and the Book*, time in his poetry assumes a more dramatic role when it functions implicitly. For this reason, I begin with a consideration of "Childe Roland to the Dark Tower Came," a poem that continues to be the accepted measure of the poet's unique world and innermost self. Having established a conceptual framework, I move to an examination of its foundation in the relatively neglected early poems, particularly that crucial cornerstone, *Sordello*. I then trace Browning's thematic and stylistic refinements in some of the most notable poems of the middle years, concluding with *The Ring*. The exclusion of particular works, and of the body of the later poetry, is not intended to imply any sort of aesthetic judgment. I have sought to examine those poems that would best represent and clarify Browning's way of meaning throughout his entire oeuvre.

Undoubtedly, the longstanding complaint against Browning that he is "obscure" is less a commentary on the poetry than on readers' requirements that meaning be reasonably stable and complete. Now, with the impact of Jacques Derrida and "deconstructionist" criticism, such lingering objections to Browning would appear to have met their match. Derrida's insistence that texts be viewed not as spatial entities but as temporal events acquires particular force in relation to a poet such as Browning, whose love of the free play of language and full awareness of the temporality of experience might qualify him as an explicit illustration of the elements Derrida finds implicit in all literature. Unlike the radical skepticism of Derrida, however, Browning's poetic faith embraces the meaning of human life, even if such meaning is to be perpetually reached for rather than conclusively grasped. More importantly, Browning's poetry has nothing to do with deconstruction's distrust of intuitive knowledge or its emphasis on the discontinuous nature of time, seen simply as the endless deferring of presence. Consequently, the discussion on time in the following chapters takes as a starting point the thought of Henri Bergson, whose profound influence on the early modern movement in literature can not detract from his usefulness in illuminating the work of a closely related progenitor.

The preoccupation of much early criticism with the philosophical teachings, or mere ideas, of Browning too often demonstrated the low yield of such approaches. The present study, while avoiding any isolated discussion of Browning as thinker, makes no apologies for its frequent recourse to Browning's thought as embodied in the dynamic network of figurative signs and enacted in the fluid language of poetic discourse. If our century has deprived Browning of his philosopher's bays, it has lessened neither the integrity of his aesthetic world nor the intensity and pertinence of his moral vision. Much of the unrest characteristic of this century can be traced to its self-consciousness concerning time. The youth who refuses to acknowledge the reality of the past and clings obstinately to a knife-edge present, the adult who refuses to accept the implication of the present and lives in the past — both equally resist the passage of time. As a corrective to such delusions, Browning's poetry discloses a world of undivided continuity and ceaseless becoming, a world of duration in which the individual retains continuity with the past and has power to shape the future.

CHAPTER I

The Test of Time:
The Browning Self

I

No discussion of time in the nineteenth century can afford to ignore the philosophy of Henri Bergson, even though it is not influential until the very end of the century. Bergson, who has been called the first philosopher to take time "seriously,"[1] that is, the first to stress its creative, mental character, and the one man to whom is chiefly due the importance of time in modern thought, represents the philosophical statement of much that had been occurring in literature throughout the century.[2] The understanding of time as "duration," Jerome Buckley admits, "belongs to a Bergsonian, post-Victorian period" but "its terms were freely anticipated" by poets and novelists throughout the nineteenth century.[3]

There are sufficient parallels to suggest that no English poet in the nineteenth century anticipated Bergson's philosophy more fully than Robert Browning. Of course, subjective time-consciousness was prevalent among the English Romantic poets, who developed creative uses of the memory to express the feeling of duration and to recapture the sense of a unified self.[4] But while others were delving into the personal past in search of a link with the present, Browning was persistently fascinated with the creative possibilities of the movement of time itself. It is in this fascination that Browning anticipates Bergson's *la durée*, which is a creative process, a ceaseless becoming. Before the feeling for time in Browning's poetry is considered, then, it will be helpful to examine briefly some major aspects of Bergson's formulation.

Bergson bases his philosophy on a fundamental dualism between spirit and matter, from which arises a corresponding opposition between time and space, intuition and intellect. Spirit is incarnate within but clearly separate from matter, which is no more than a symbolic representation of the real life of things. The common tendency of us all, according to Bergson, is to substitute for the reality the mere symbol. The intellect is so accustomed to measuring inert matter in space that it falls into the habit of applying the same quantitative criteria to time. Consequently, we come to accept the ticks of the clock, the instants ranged alongside each other in homogeneous space, as part of reality rather than as a practical convenience. Enabled by the intellect to establish a toe-hold in the world of flux, we soon come to base our knowledge of reality on the external evidence we ourselves have provided. We believe our mental states to exist concurrently with the ticks of the clock. If, however, we "ask consciousness to isolate itself from the external world" and "to become itself again,"[5] we will discover that "states of consciousness, even when successive, permeate one another, and [that] in the simplest of them the whole soul can be reflected."[6] Thus we are led to see that real time, or *durée réelle*, is an indivisible flow of successive but totally interpenetrating parts. Such a view rejects the conception of time as a line, on which a before and after can be distinguished as well as past, present and future. Instead, all of the past is constantly transmuted into the onward movement of the present; nothing is ever lost, for like a growing snowball the present is always filled up with the past. Bergson, in a characteristic and frequently quoted passage, says, "Duration is the continuous progress of the past which gnaws into the future and which swells as it advances."[7]

This projection of the past into the present causes memory to acquire a new meaning. Since our present character is the synthesis of all our past states, we perceive only the past, the present being nothing more than reality in the making, an opportunity to act with regard to the future. Thus, memory becomes identical with consciousness itself. There is no need for the retrospective glance which would close the gap with the past, for the absence of a time line insures against such an interruption, or spatial image, ever occurring. Bergson warns that memory "is not a faculty of putting away recollections in a drawer."[8] The individual "who lives in the past for the mere pleasure of living there" is "but a dreamer."[9]

Even though the whole past is automatically preserved to bear upon our actions in the present, we should become mere creatures of habit if we relied on this form of memory alone. Lest we base our actions purely on impulse, there is a second, independent memory, which is composed of images related to time and place. Its function is to "complete and illuminate the present situation with a view to ultimate action."[10] Though spontaneous and initially retrospective, this memory is not related to associationism, which substitutes for the "continuity of becoming, which is the living reality, a discontinuous multiplicity of elements, inert and juxtaposed."[11] Instead, the images of the independent memory enable us to retrace the movement of the first memory until it materializes in a present action. Bergson's concept of memory, then, discourages all forms of nostalgia by constantly leading us to a present that

13

already contains the totality of the past. This fullness of the present is described in terms especially applicable to Robert Browning's own concern with the present moment: " . . . the present . . . seems constantly to be starting afresh; and we . . . see ourselves in the instantaneous, speak of the past as something done away with, and see in memory a fact strange or in any case foreign to us, an aid given to mind by matter. Let us on the contrary grasp ourselves afresh as we are, in a present which is thick, and furthermore, elastic, which we can stretch indefinitely backwards by pushing the screen which masks us from ourselves farther and farther away . . . "[12]

Bergson repeatedly urges us to get back into the deep and fundamental self rather than remain bound to its symbolic substitute. We are free only when we recover ourselves, and the moments at which we may do so are rare. In order to grasp the real self in its flowing through time, we must rely on intuition. The intellect, which is capable only of dealing with objects in space and representing them by stable concepts, is wholly inadequate to the task. Intuition, on the other hand, rejects conceptual representations and urges that we place ourselves "within an object in order to coincide with what is unique in it and consequently inexpressible."[13] By installing itself in the moving, intuition enables us to attain the world of *durée* and the real self.

Once we uncover the living, developing self we discover that freedom is a clear fact. Determinism and predestination apply strictly to time which has passed rather than to time passing. Only in the latter does the self *endure*, not as a completed act but as a continuous process. Principles of cause and effect and concepts of finalism result when we represent psychological states in space, according to a time line, and fail to recognize their successive interpenetration in duration. In reality, or in the world of *durée*, we are free to create ourselves endlessly, each act being an expression of our whole past, which shares in, but does not cause, the present action. We cannot think of this creative process, or express it in concepts, without misrepresenting and destroying it. Through intuition, however, we can *experience* it as a vital impulse flowing through all things and uniting all to the same life force. Real time is identical with this force — a creative, spiritual movement renewing itself indefinitely and increasing as it goes on.

We do not live so much in time, then, as time lives in us. We are the incarnation of time; our actions both express and create its movement within us. Our only chance to experience this creative impulse and to act freely is through intuition, "a lamp almost extinguished, which glimmers now and then." It is these "fleeting intuitions," Bergson says, which "philosophy ought to seize"[14] so that it may guide us to the life of spirit.

Robert Browning had already seized these momentary intuitions as the subject of poetry. In "Abt Vogler" the extemporizing composer realizes for an ecstatic instant the impulse that binds all to one cosmic unity: "For earth had attained to heaven, there was no near nor far" (32).[15] Not only is space banished, but future and present come together in the same moment of intuitive insight: "What never had been was now; what was, as it shall be anon..." (39). Paracelsus is another Browning visionary who briefly glimpses the dynamic spiritual reality when just prior to his death he is made to see that "progress is / The law of life..." (742-43). Time no longer represents a threat to the old values, for the movement of time has taken value unto itself, revealing a God of vital energy.

Written nearly thirty years after the youthful and romantic *Paracelsus*, the "Epilogue" to *Dramatis Personae*, which gives us Browning's mature beliefs in religion and philosophy, shows that Browning's attitude toward time — while it has deepened and become more resolute through experience — remains essentially unchanged. Renan, the rational, liberal Christian, is led to despairing skepticism when he sees that the idea of a permanent and personal God cannot be reconciled with modern science. The "star" (24) once thought permanent and the "Face" (26) which seemed to express human love, disappear when addressed "to motion" (37), leaving man totally desolate in a world controlled by natural law.

Browning, in his rebuke to Renan, refuses to view nature as a mechanical system indifferent, or even hostile, toward human nature. Instead, the mobility that is in nature is identical with the dynamic spiritual power that is in man. It sweeps over man, who is "king / O' the current for a minute" (81-82), but in doing so it shows its end is "to enhance / His worth" (89-90). The onward movement of time, "old yet ever new" (94), isolates each human being and sustains a "strife" (91) of which the individual's life is the final "product" (90). It is in time that the individual experiences spiritual growth while the immanent and vital nature of God is being evolved throughout the universe. The Face, which once seemed to desert the poet, now evolves with him:

> That one Face, far from vanish, rather grows,
> Or decomposes but to recompose,
> Become my universe that feels and knows. (99-101)

The challenge of time, to which Renan had responded negatively, elicits a positive statement of faith from Browning. The once stable and permanent value yields to the force of time so that it may *become* something in greater harmony with human needs and aspirations. No longer confined to Temple, the incarnate Spirit becomes incarnate within the whole universe.

The dualism in Browning is not so much in the nature of things as in the perception of them. It is the intellect which forces a diametric opposition between the world of spirit and the world of nature where in reality there is harmony. The entire universe is the incarnation of a God who is not pure spirit, merely, but a vital dynamic force. From this conviction perceived through intuition, Browning is able to begin with an understanding of time and nature which persistently eluded Arnold and Tennyson. Of the two possible views of nature which Arnold offers in "In Utrumque Paratus" — on the one hand an animate, purposeful nature, and on the other a soulless, mechanistic nature — it is the latter which dominates his poetry. Unable to effect a reconciliation between humanity and nature, Arnold abruptly finds that his poetic vision darkens, as it yields to a universe of frozen apathy:

> ... I alone
> Am dead to life and joy, therefore I read
> In all things my own deadness.   (*Empedocles on Etna*, II. 320-22)[16]

Even Tennyson can find no more than tentative evidence of a spiritual power in nature. Assigned to the lower sphere of the physical and the transitory, nature is indifferent, and often hostile — "red in tooth and claw" (*In Memoriam*, LVI) — toward human good. Only after the individual has defied change and transcended time to embrace the spiritual stability of a higher life, is it possible to see "That all, as in some piece of art, / Is toil cooperant to an end" (*In Memoriam*, CXXVIII).[17]

For Browning, "heaven's high" and "earth's low" so "intertwine" ("Epilogue," 67) that direct intuition of a divine spirit is attained not by defying time but by immersing oneself in its transforming flux. As in Bergsonian duration, time is a creative process, a continuous becoming which evolves through humans and all finite things. In "The Englishman in Italy," a frequently anthologized but nonetheless overlooked nature poem, the poet attains a summit from which he may view the whole:

> And God's own profound
> Was above me, and round me the mountains,
> And under, the sea,
> And within me my heart to bear witness
> What was and shall be.   (172-76)

The past and future are contained in the same infinite moment, which retains the dynamic motion of the world below him — "Oh, those mountains, their infinite movement! / Still moving with you" (181-82) — for he discovers that the silence of the mountains is not to be mistaken for indifference to human actions. All is part of a larger but single, unified process, realized for a passionate instant at the height of his ascent. In a flash of insight the gap between mind and universe has been bridged; the poet sees that all nature is derived of one source, a single cosmic movement of which human life is a manifestation.

Suddenly, the intuitive moment is over, and the poet descends reluctantly from the dynamic world of duration to the static world of space, where the myth-making activities of the human intellect proceed to oppress the free human spirit. The occasion is the "feast of the Rosary's Virgin" and no efforts have been spared to prepare the church "for the show" (248) — from gaudy paper decorations to a scaffold "Rigged glorious to hold / All the fiddlers and fifers and drummers / And trumpeters bold" (262-64), not to mention the highlight of the show, the "flaxen-wigged Image" (269), which is to be paraded about by stomping priests and then saluted with the explosions of gunpowder-filled bottles. The poet is unable to regard such fatuous behavior sympathetically. Just as the priests are vain and foolish in their irreverent representations of the evolving power in the universe, legislators in England are equally given to self-delusion when they sanction unnatural, oppressive laws:

>   — "Such trifles!" you say?
> Fortu, in my England at home,
>   Men meet gravely to-day
> And debate, if abolishing Corn-laws
>   Be righteous and wise
> — If 't were proper, Scirocco should vanish
>   In black from the skies!   (286-92)

In other words, the conservative few, with pretense to wisdom and good judgment, should have no more power to deny human progress than to stop the process that is at work throughout nature. Having viewed the transforming power in the world and experienced its irresistible force, the poet can treat presumptuousness with impatient sarcasm.

Since it is only through inner consciousness that nature can be experienced as interpenetrating flow, Browning's natural settings are usually symbolic of the way the mind works and are not, simply, complements to the mind's activities. His landscapes tend to elude the mind's eye, preventing it from retaining a set picture of any particular scene. The "spots of time," which landscape often creates in Wordsworth's memory, are rare in Browning. He has no need to close the gap with the past, for memory preserves

17

the past in the present and consequently shares in the forward movement of the present.

This personal understanding of time is perhaps no more strongly felt than in "Childe Roland," a poem in which, as most critics agree, Browning expressed the innermost pattern of his mind. The widely recognized subjectivity of the poem has led to a diversity of interpretations, although most critics, in agreeing that the poem is somehow a revelation of the Browning self, are tacitly acknowledging that " 'Childe Roland to the Dark Tower Came' " is principally about time. Time is the very condition for the sense of a continuous and unified self, and the poem reveals, in the flow of consciousness which it records, a self-in-process. Any purpose or meaning which the individual may claim comes as a result of the response to temporal flow. The individual may vainly try to stop the flux, despair before its unrelenting, destructive force, or find in it the potential for creation and spiritual development. This is the test of time; each individual creates a self by his or her response to it.

Recent criticism has been inclined to accept Browning's insistence that he had no allegorical intentions in writing "Childe Roland" and that the poem came upon him "as a kind of dream."[18] Robert Langbaum in *The Poetry of Experience* supports this idea in his approach to the poem: "The details of the poem are not allegorical just because they are not representative of an idea but of a perception. They are evocative — used to make us see what the knight sees, so we can respond as he does and thus participate in his growth of consciousness."[19] Beyond this Langbaum does not go; the meaning of the poem is simply "what the speaker both reveals and discovers about himself."[20] But since the "what" remains totally without referent, it becomes difficult finally to see how we are enabled to participate in the poem.

Langbaum's reserve is understandable in view of the contrived Freudian analyses and rigid moral schemes interpreters have frequently imposed on the poem.[21] Of all the specific readings, Harold Bloom's progressively refined and provocative argument is the one to be reckoned with. Bloom's preoccupation with the poem in four closely sequenced books is based on the identification of Shelley as "the poem's pervasive subject, the betrayed ideal whose spirit haunts Roland."[22] What Roland finally sees is that he can neither rise to the eminence of his poetic forebear nor conclusively repress him and invent his own imaginative father. The reader's involvement in the poem, then, may be attributed to the need to become one's own imaginative father, one's own begotten son, alternative ways of describing the widely shared quest for an autonomous self.

Bloom's interpretation of *Childe Roland* is frequently illuminating, even apart from its accompanying theory of poetic influence. Let us for the moment, however, drop the identification of the poem's subject with Shelley and see what specific inferences can be drawn directly from the poem. Actually, the speaker is himself quite clear in describing the circumstances preceding the quest and in revealing the state of his mind. The "hoary cripple" (2) who points the way certainly personifies debilitating old age, or death itself, gleeful to gain "one more victim" (6). The speaker relates that his search has lasted for years and that his hope has dwindled into nothing. Once confident and optimistic in his quest, he is now clearly disillusioned and suspects deceit and treachery on the part of the old man. He can no longer anticipate the approaching end with joy or a sense of fulfillment but suspects the old cripple has fed him "lies" (8). In a spirit of futility and resignation, Childe Roland accepts the directions that are given him and sets off on the path to the Dark Tower. The question for him is no longer whether he will succeed where all his predecessors failed, but simply whether his failure will be as noble, or distinguished, as theirs. Once he has committed himself to renewing the quest, there is no turning back. The very road on which he had come has vanished and left him a prisoner of the blighted, desolate plain.

All of this information is given us in the first nine stanzas of the poem, before the hero even begins his journey across the wasteland. We learn that the hero has suffered profound disillusionment over the value of his quest and given up all hope of success. We can infer that success does not consist merely in finding the Dark Tower. Hidden by an "ominous tract" (14), the Dark Tower represents some kind of test to the knights who finally confront it. All of the previous knights have failed the test and the hero now fully expects to do the same. His only hope is "that some end might be" (18). Even provided with this background, we are perhaps not justified in assigning symbolic values to each of the details of the devastated landscape which the knight travels across. But we can see that this barren, sterile nature, without precedent as far as the speaker is concerned, is consonant with the speaker's own lost hope and arrested energy. Moreover, the force that imprisons nature's regenerative power comes neither from nature nor from a divine source:

> ... said Nature peevishly,
> "It nothing skills: I cannot help my case:
> 'T is the Last Judgment's fire must cure this place,
> Calcine its clods and set my prisoners free."   (63-66)

William DeVane, surprised that Browning, who is "almost always dramatic, and whose landscapes are generally brief and entirely subservient to narrative and character," should write a poem in which "the landscape is
everything," called the quest an "interpolation into the mood of the poem."[23]
If, however, we accept the landscape as representative of the stages in the
knight's consciousness, it becomes inseparable from the quest. And, as we
have seen already, there are numerous instances in which the speaker fore-
goes the description of his surroundings in order to divulge directly his inner
feelings. In stanza XV the speaker shuts his eyes and turns them on his
heart, where he hopes to find comfort in memories of "earlier, happier
sights" (87). But the recollection of two knightly comrades who were later
disgraced convinces him that his present struggle is preferable: "Better this
present than a past like that; / Back therefore to my darkening path again!"
(103-04).

Deprived of sight and sound, he is soon filled with uncertainty and despair. A little river unexpectedly crosses his path and results in a sense of
renewed purpose, however. Since the implications of the river are strongly
suicidal, it serves as a preliminary test to the hero, affording him an opportunity to abandon his search altogether. But he sets out to ford the stream,
ignoring the "suicidal throng" (118) of drenched willows and trying his
best "not to set foot on a dead man's cheek" (122). Upon reaching the
other side he finds that circumstances have not improved and that his goal
is no nearer. He has merely proven his determination to endure until the
end.

Again the knight is surrounded by a devastated landscape, one trampled
beyond recognition by "strugglers" (129) whose brains must have been set to
work by "mad brewage" (136). Just when the hero despairs of finding an
end, however, an ominous, vulture-like bird brings to him an intuition of
the place he has been seeking. Inexplicably, the plain has given place to
mountains and the speaker berates himself as a "dunce" and a "dotard"
(178) for not immediately recognizing the sight, which has been the destina-
tion of his whole life's quest. The Dark Tower now stands before him,
threatening to destroy him but not without the cooperation of the speaker
himself. It is not an aggressive, overpowering force but simply a "round
squat turret" (182) acting as an obstructing menace in the same way that
an unseen reef imperils a ship. Moreover, the inanimate tower is "blind as
the fool's heart" (182); it is a menace in proportion to the blindness in the
human heart.

The sight and sound that were earlier denied the speaker now come to
his aid, transforming his surroundings and illuminating the moment of crisis:

Not see? because of night perhaps? — why, day
    Came back again for that! (187-88)

Not hear?   when noise was everywhere! it tolled
    Increasingly like a bell. Names in my ears
    Of all the lost adventurers my peers, — . . . .
    Lost, lost! one moment knelled the woe of years.   (193-95, 198)

The past appears in the present moment, offering to the hero the example
of the knights, his peers, who themselves failed and who now gather around
on the hillsides to see Childe Roland, a doomed "game at bay" (191), share
their fate:

> There they stood, ranged along the hill-sides, met
>   To view the last of me, a living frame
>   For one more picture! (199-201)

But in this intuitive, expanded moment the hero refuses to submit to the
past which seems to decree his inescapable destiny. Instead, he draws upon
it to illuminate his present action, which consequently expresses his whole
being, the quest itself:

> . . . in a sheet of flame
> I saw them and I knew them all. And yet
> Dauntless the slug-horn to my lips I set,
> And blew *"Childe Roland to the Dark Tower came."* (201-04)

   The knight's final act is not merely a blast of defiance but a song of
triumph. Harold Bloom, while acknowledging the triumphant surge with
which the poem ends, locates the power of the poem in its record of creative
failure. For Bloom the poet-quester's attempt to revise the past places him
in a struggle with time which, though futile, enables Roland to manifest
poetic strength and attain a kind of heroic, tragic grandeur.[24] This description of Roland would be more satisfying were it applied to Browning's Paracelsus, whose ruined quest produces visionary clairvoyance. But *Childe
Roland* is a later poem, revealing at once the evolution of the poet and the
rite of passage of the hero. The Knight does not come before the tower and
simply await its deathblow in response to his challenge. His victory is sig-
nalled by his use of the past tense: " 'Childe Roland to the Dark Tower
came.' " The "childe," the young, untested knight, has proven himself a
worthy knight by passing the test; now he may continue on his quest.
   The Tower, then, is both an obstacle and an opportunity, for only by
confronting it does the speaker achieve the self-revelation which enables him
to go on. Specifically, the Tower represents the test of time — Childe Roland
may, as his predecessors did, despair before the destructive forces in the uni-

verse and succumb; or he may, by acting, realize the potential of these forces for his unending development.[25] Whenever the knight seeks to retreat in time, or to find comfort in memories, he narrowly escapes the fate of his comrades. By his climactic action, however, he gathers into unity the totality of his past experience, permitting it to share in the creation of the future. Thus, the experience which leads to the transformation of the speaker's vision is itself transformed to agree with the speaker's new awareness. Langbaum describes this reciprocal action as a pattern which operates on two levels: "Since the knight makes the pattern by *seeing* the landscape as vibrating with significance, he stands in the same relation to the poem as the poet in that he finds in the circumstances the Song which he himself has brought to them."[26] In other words, the pattern not only is *in* the poem but *is* the poem. This pattern, as Langbaum suggests, approximates the non-verbal expressive nature of music. By itself the knight's blast means little as an idea, yet in its integral relation to the whole it means everything that the poem by its movement expresses.

Of course, music, which expresses emotion through primary symbols, can not completely account for the pattern of literary meaning in poetry. The specific pattern expressed in "Childe Roland" is one of *duration*. The knight passes through a world in which man has cut up flowing time into a dead, static landscape reflecting his own sterility. At the critical moment, the landscape of the poem undergoes a transformation as does the consciousness of the hero, for past experience has been transmuted into his present consciousness. Time now exists *in* him as duration; all experience is included in an indivisible stream which manifests itself in new, creative acts.

Browning's insistence that "Childe Roland" came upon him as a "kind of dream" should not be lightly regarded. It is in dream, Bergson emphasizes, that "we no longer measure duration, but we feel it."[27] Contributing to the final dream effect, or sense of duration, is Browning's exclusive use of the past tense. We are not strongly aware of an objective time sequence because the point of view of the speaker places the events in an indeterminate past. Since the speaker's act — the utterance of the Song — is no more than a précis of all that has gone before as well as a completion of it, the events of the poem all seem contingent upon, if not inseparable from, this one culminating moment of action. But there is another important result — almost directly contrary to the dream effect — which Browning secures through his use of the past tense. The poem has an unmistakably present-tense effect despite the past-tense form. Had Browning related the events of the poem in the present tense, however, they would have assumed the elusive quality of sheer fantasy. Lacking Browning's usual careful objective setting, the narrative achieves a semblance of reality because the experience has just taken place in the immediate past. In large part, then, the present tense involvement which the reader experiences is *because* of the past tense form.

For Langbaum the disparity between the immediacy of the utterance and the past tense of the situation indicates a split in the knight's person. It enables us to understand that "the knight is directing his utterance outward to a projection of himself," that he is, in effect, conducting a "dialogue with himself."[28] If so, it is a unified, concrete self, and not a projection or a split ego, that emerges alone to proclaim its victory. The process is the same as that described by Bergson: "The greater part of the time we live outside ourselves ... perceiving our own ghost, a colorless shadow. ... Hence our life unfolds in space rather than in time; we live for the external world rather than for ourselves ... we 'are acted' rather than act ourselves. To act freely is to recover possession of oneself, and to get back into pure duration."[29]

CHAPTER II

The Knife-Edge Present

Pauline, Paracelsus and *Sordello* have generally been regarded as fruitful failures in Browning's development as a dramatic poet. The confessional nature of the poems, while problematic to structure and technique, permitted the young follower of Shelley to see the dangers of an unbridled romantic egoism and to make the adjustments which would lead to personal and artistic maturity. The problem explored in these early monodramas is the need to break free of self-isolating subjectivity and establish an effectual relation with communal life; the common theme of all three poems is identical with that expressed in Browning's later poetry: the challenge of fitting the infinite to the finite.[1] Each character experiences boundless aspiration and grandiose, Promethean ambitions but is unable to reconcile his inexhaustible demands and insatiable cravings with the conditions and limitations of mundane existence.

Time is a predicament for the idealistic hero of each of the poems because it constantly seems to frustrate the realization of his lofty goals. The tradition of the past is ever an oppressive burden to him, mocking his attempt to ignore its precedent and effect immediate reforms. The movement of the present also confounds him, for he feels that time is constantly running out before he can put his plans into effect. Unable to find value in the past or continuity in the present moment, each protagonist discovers himself the victim of a knife-edge present, in which he is in constant danger of being obliterated as one instant is erased by the next. Failing to understand the creative possibilities in the movement of time itself, Browning's early heroes become engaged in a futile contest with time. They fail because, like Sordello, each is "alone / Quite out of Time and this world" (VI, 485-86).[2]

Unlike Childe Roland, whose skepticism ultimately discovers a pattern of coherent meaning, these confident questers surrender their paths to chaotic forces that diffuse and threaten to dissolve the meaning of their tests and texts. Nevertheless, a consecutive reading of the poems reveals the poet gradually acquiring strength in the conviction that to ignore the claims of the temporal is to evade life's test and to fall into isolation and spiritual abstraction. The poet's struggle to combat this stasis and to achieve a more fully developed, human self along with an organic literary form for expressing it, places these poems, despite their flaws and incomprehensibilities, among the most immediate and self-revealing works Browning ever wrote.

I

Browning's later comment on his first published effort that "good draughtmanship . . . and right handling were beyond the artist at that time"[3] is only partially satisfactory in explaining the poem's deficiencies. Brilliant in parts, *Pauline* ultimately breaks down due to a failure of conception rather than technique. The youthful imagination that is responsible for the immediacy of the inner life presented by the poem is not sufficiently powerful to resolve, or even lend a sense of importance to, the various dilemmas which the poem sets forth. Nevertheless, some recent critical efforts have been made to rescue *Pauline* from the severe strictures it initially received, especially from John Stuart Mill. There is the temptation to see in the poem a passage to emotional and poetic maturity because the speaker, despairing and guilt-ridden as he calls to Pauline in the opening lines of the poem, announces in the concluding lines that he is free of doubt and fear. Yet as Mill astutely observed, the intended resolution is far from convincing. Amid the confused and fluctuating moods that are recorded, no clear transformation in the speaker's consciousness ever occurs. There appears to be no significant difference, finally, between the moments which open and close the poem.

Pauline is written in the present tense, except for a narrative interlude in which the poet-speaker gives a history of his soul. Dissatisfied with his present accomplishments, he wishes at once to erase the disappointment of the immediate past and to retreat to a congenial distant past. Failing at both, he seeks to sever himself completely from the past by returning to a present that is timeless and unreal. The abrupt shifts in tense thus mirror the speaker's unsettled state of mind.

Initially the poet-hero suffers from a vague sense of guilt which causes him to seek a return to Pauline and to the hope and purpose he once knew in life. His crime, as he sees it, was that in pursuing his "wild dreams of beauty and of good" (30) he had set himself in opposition to the conditions prescribed by God and nature. But though he expresses disillusionment and bitter shame, the dominant note in his complaint is one of disappointment rather than penitence. He declares that he can be young again simply by giving up all he has aspired toward and returning to blissful memories of youth. Not only the speaker's escapist attitude toward time but his continuing adulation of Shelley, the idol of his youth, confirms his complacent position. In a glowing tribute to the "Sun-treader" (141-229) he continues to

25

uphold the life of the poet who shaped the early romantic ideals to which he has just attributed his present misery. His closing plea to Shelley mirrors regret and self-pity rather than remorse or self-understanding: "Remember me who praise thee e'en with tears, / For never more shall I walk calm with thee ... " (219-20).

Shelley's calmness throughout the poem serves as a foil to the speaker's agitation, a difference which the speaker ironically tries to exploit to his personal advantage. If Shelley has attained a transcendent tranquility exempting him from earthly vicissitude, the speaker would at least enlist our sympathy for the plight of his abandoned follower, left behind to struggle valiantly in a lower, mutable realm. But the speaker's dislocation of the present from the past defeats his efforts to come to terms with the temporal order. His defiance of succession, on the one hand, permits him to reverse the temporal circumstances of his relationship with Shelley, who is enjoined to "remember" the descendant, but on the other hand, it continually intrudes upon his claims of self-autonomy.

Having rejected his past endeavors as "valueless" and sensing that all present efforts are tainted and ineffectual, the speaker nevertheless maintains the existence of a unique identity, "Of self, distinct from all its qualities" (270) and linked to a creative impulse which would rule, know and experience all. In the spirit of recent phenomenological accounts of schizophrenia,[4] he experiences his inner, "true" self as divorced from his outer, "false" self. Although this unembodied self seeks omnipotence, its isolation from the outer world leads to a sense of impoverishment and despair. The speaker attributes his isolation to a temporal discontinuity, blaming the failure of his creative potential on the past, which he bids Pauline to forget "as a sad sick dream!" (244). Rather than absorb the lesson of the past and allow it to contribute to his development in the present, he regarded it as a challenge to his own fancied preeminence:

> I rather sought
> To rival what I wondered at than form
> Creations of my own. (390-92)

The theme of the challenger is for Browning associated with the poet's anxiety over the past. The later, younger poet may choose or reject the influence of the prior temporal claim or transform it through an act of creative renewal. At the climax of *Sordello* the narrator readmits Eglamor, a dismissed rival poet, in order to overcome petty rivalry and rejoin past with present. The speaker of *Pauline*, unfortunately, can not surmount adolescent egoism. Whenever the past challenged his need for priority, he

took the escapist route: "Let fancy bear me / Far from the past!" (477-78).
He soon discovered, however, that the severance of the past from the present
caused the present moment to contract, making it a point without duration.
His only hope against the debilitating movement of time, he came to believe,
was to cling to this brief instant and enjoy it while he might:

> . . . I had resolved
> No Age should come on me ere youth was spent,
> For I would wear myself out, like that morn
> Which wasted not a sunbeam; every hour
> I would make mine, and die. (500-04)

The speaker's decadent reliance on the isolated instant distinguishes him
from Shelley's stable repose, yet it is not a contrast that permits him to establish a separate poetic identity. Despite the submission of his early Shelleyan
ideals to the hostile movement of time, his worshipful attitude toward
Shelley remains unchanged. In the speaker's view, Shelley, like himself, had
defied time, and an obstinate adulation of Shelley indicates that the speaker's
disillusionment is incomplete, his penitence far from sincere:

> 'Nought makes me trust some love is true,
> But the delight of the contented lowness
> With which I gaze on him I keep for ever
> Above me; I to rise and rival him?
> Feed his fame rather from my heart's best blood,
> Wither unseen that he may flourish still.' (554-59)

The initial genuflection meant to express the speaker's indebtedness to his
poetic father is suddenly turned upside down. Unable to "rise and rival"
Shelley, the speaker in the last two lines simply lowers Shelley to the mutable order, making the forerunner's fame dependent upon the speaker's
efforts. Though the poet-hero is consistently adept at self-deception, the
reader should not be similarly deceived. The recurring posture of humility
— whether toward Shelley, Pauline, or God — is in each instance, a form of
self-vindication.

Abandoning the history of self and once more addressing Pauline in the
present tense, the speaker repeats his conviction that the creative impulse he
experiences is necessarily incompatible with finite existence, which demands
the imprisonment of all such impulses:

> I cannot chain my soul: it will not rest
> In its clay prison, this most narrow sphere;
> It has strange impulse, tendency, desire,
> Which nowise I account for nor explain,
> But cannot stifle, being bound to trust

27

> All feelings equally, to hear all sides:
> How can my life indulge them?   (593-99)

The answer to this Faustian question, the speaker is convinced, cannot be found in the temporal world. Frustrated that he must remain "this vile form's slave" (617) and that even love "Perforce receives its object from this earth" (638), he favors his reason and its abstractions, which time can in no way affect. Despising the earthly elements of his being, he directs his passion not to a live person but to Andromeda, the subject of a painting, for "change can touch her not" (658). Although powerless to resist the force of change himself, he is confident that death will provide a release from time. He will "triumph through decay" (675), thus permitting his "wondrous mind" (669) to become unencumbered of finite existence.

Just as a need for self-vindication had driven the speaker to renew his childhood worship of Shelley, he now weakly imagines a love for Pauline, so that he will not "be left / Utterly loveless" (690-91). There is no question that the speaker's love is another of his "wild fancies," totally abstracted from the temporal order. With Pauline, he is "As one breathing his weakness to the ear / Of pitying angel" (710-11); not surprisingly his message is equally disembodied and unreal:

> Pauline, come with me, see how I could build
> A home for us, out of the world, in thought!
> I am uplifted: fly with me, Pauline!   (729-31)

Despite these frantic flights of fancy, the speaker is again brought back to an inescapable, painful awareness of time and change: "But my soul saddens when it looks beyond: / I cannot be immortal, taste all joy" (809-10). His frustrating search for images of fixity, which led him to embrace Shelley, Andromeda and Pauline, now causes him to direct his attentions to a more permanent figure:

> And what is it that I hunger for but God?
> My God, my God, let me for once look on thee
> As though nought else existed, we alone!   (821-23)

The forced repetitions of the word "God" signal the contrivance whereby the hero imagines yet another solipsist relationship. Previously he had indicated that a tendency of his soul toward God was a defense against the destructive activities of time, and his reaffirmation of this escapist position, though an immediate source of comfort to him, hardly suggests a satisfying resolution of his conflict with temporal existence. Even his reference to the death and resurrection of Christ (849-54) turns out to be another of his "wandering dreams" (848) rather than an acceptance of his humanity.

28

Despite the speaker's insistence that he now discerns "Faintly how life is truth and truth is good" (888), a persistent selfishness prevents him from seeing beyond his own disappointment.[5] He addresses Pauline in the same self-pathetic manner with which he had earlier addressed Shelley: "I stained myself / But to behold thee purer by my side . . . " (905-06).

Thus Pauline is a defense mechanism, a weak prop for his ego,[6] which now loses its last opportunity to come to terms with the temporal order: "No more of the past! I'll look within no more" (937). Declaring himself love's slave, the speaker attempts to fly away with Pauline once more, avoiding all "That tells of the past doubt" (971). Any obstacle they might encounter in their flight will be regarded simply as "a dream which death will dissipate" (979). Thus the speaker concludes on a note of decadence and futility. Though he attempts to divorce himself from the past and from time, he remains time's subject; he cannot deny that "ere the cold morning all [may] be gone" (987). All he has is a tenuous claim to "this moment's pride" (993) and the fanciful hope that when his elaborate conceit with Pauline is shattered he can again retreat to abstract realms and live with poets. In a closing tribute to Shelley the speaker reaffirms his obstinate attachment to his idol, whose permanence is invoked to cast a heroic light upon the speaker's immanent destruction:

> . . . I seem, dying, as one going in the dark
> To fight a giant: but live thou for ever,
> And be to all what thou hast been to me!   (1026-28)

Though the dying quester in these lines bears a superficial resemblance to Childe Roland, the hero of *Pauline* is far from being a giant killer. The giant that he jousts with but fails to vanquish, that his ambivalence will not allow him to dethrone, is the figure of Shelley. Whether the documented allusions in *Pauline* to such poems as *Alastor, Epipsychidion,* and *Adonais*[7] are deliberate revisions or derivative adaptations is less important than the poet's persistent entanglement with his idol. The predecessor poet's contests with time are simply held up to contrast with and provide a warrant for the speaker's own fated endeavors.

Browning is said to have related once that it was Judas Iscariot's intense faith in Christ that led to betrayal of the father figure.[8] In *Pauline* the poet's identification with Shelley provokes introspective questioning about the attachment but stops considerably short of betrayal. The ability to make such a separation would not occur until later years when Browning, in describing Shelley as dying "before his youth ended," would refer to the whole

29

of Shelley's poetry as a sublime "fragmentary essay"[9] and to his own *Pauline* as a "boyish work," a "crude preliminary sketch."[10]

Recent critics have tended to override Browning's disclaimers as well as Mill's strictures by insisting that the poet achieves a satisfying resolution in *Pauline*.[11] Yet Mill's criticism remains one of the most perceptive comments on the conclusion of the poem: "A cento of most beautiful passages might be made from this poem, and the psychological history of himself is powerful and truthful — *truth-like* certainly, all but the last stage. *That*, he evidently has not yet got into. . . . Meanwhile he should not attempt to show how a person may be *recovered* from this morbid state — for *he* is hardly convalescent, and 'what should we speak of but that which we know?' "[12] It seems hardly fair to expect that Browning, at the age of twenty, should have resolved the conflict between the ideals of an adolescent, romantic temperament and the limits of a finite, mutable existence. It is sufficiently remarkable that in his next major poem, *Paracelsus*, he would offer a clear resolution to the conflict that had occupied him just two years earlier.

II

Pauline's lover was the victim of a youthful pride which distorted his view of the past. Choosing first to rival the past, then to replace it with his own accomplishments and, failing this, to ignore it altogether, he is reduced finally to a pathetic dependence on a fragile, durationless instant. The idealistic hero is a loser in his contest with time, frustrated equally by a fixed past and an unstable present. The problem that occupied Browning in *Pauline* — how to realize the imagination's towering conceptions within the temporal conditions of life — again provides the central theme in *Paracelsus*. Here Browning expands upon the theme, exploring it in exhaustive detail before allowing the hero a death-bed revelation of the truth which reconciles him with human existence. Though a diffuse and static poem through its first four cantos, *Paracelsus* repays attentive reading because in it Browning introduces the major ideas and convictions that inform all of his later poetry.

Browning's preface to the first edition of the poem describes his method: " . . . instead of having recourse to an external machinery of incidents to create and evolve the crisis I desire to produce, I have ventured to display somewhat minutely the mood itself in its rise and progress, and have suffered the agency by which it is influenced and determined to be generally discernible in its effects alone. . . . "[13] The explanation might be interpreted as an apology for the distinctly undramatic nature of the poem. In Canto I

Paracelsus aspires, and in the remaining four cantos he is occupied with understanding the reason for his failure, an action which is never presented. The inevitability of failure can be inferred, however, from Paracelsus' pronouncements in the opening canto, in which he informs his friends, Festus and Michal, of the divine commission he has received to save mankind. Alarmed by Paracelsus' God-like presumption, Festus urges him to pursue "approved example" (I. 385) and to converse with "the great dead" (386). But Paracelsus persists in his belief that the accumulated learning of the past belongs to the "outward things" (727) which produce ignorance. Maintaining that "Truth is within ourselves" (726), he exposes his own ignorance by embracing an intransigent dualism in which truth is a mysterious "splendor" (735), a "radiance vast" (740) struggling to escape from the "perverting carnel mesh" (732) which imprisons it.

The greatest obstacle which Paracelsus thinks he must overcome before he may free his soul and release its truth is time:

> See this soul of ours!
> How it strives weakly in the child, is loosed
> In manhood, clogged by sickness, back compelled
> By age and waste, set free at last by death.... (I. 759-62)

This cynical little speech depicting human life as retrogressive is the exact opposite of Paracelsus's concluding speech, which will introduce an evolutionary, progressive scheme. As yet, however, Paracelsus has no plan for dealing with time, other than to confront it with Shelleyan defiance. Buoyed by his idealistic visions and transported by pride, he first orders God to "elevate the race at once" (780) and then, practically in the same breath, issues a reckless challenge: "See if we cannot beat thine angels yet!" (784). By Canto II, already disillusioned over his quest, he seeks to understand the reason for its failure. Time, which had been a threat from the beginning, now serves as an obvious scapegoat. Self-piteously Paracelsus acknowledges the old adage, " 'Time fleets, youth fades, life is an empty dream' " (II. 43, 53). All he can hope for is that time will quickly run out, bringing "An end, a rest" (66). Unable to accept personal responsibility for his failure, he directs his resentment toward God, though this childish maneuver is readily exposed by his choice of language:

> At worst I have performed my share of the task:
> The rest is God's concern; mine, merely this,
> To know that I have obstinately held
> By my own work. (II. 90-93)

Self-righteous and intractable, Paracelsus is willing to consider only one shortcoming on his part — the possibility that his pursuit of knowledge has caused him to neglect love. It remains to be seen, through the character of Aprile, whether this deficiency in itself accounts for his failure. As a youth subject to the claims of love, Paracelsus had been able to regard life, death and all nature's shows as the "bare receptacles / Or indices of truth" (157-58), a single truth equally present in all earthly phenomena. As the proud and ambitious reformer of Canto I, however, he had rejected "outward things" as needless distractions to the truth which is solely "within ourselves." The result is that Paracelsus now finds himself the victim of a profound paradox. Instead of gaining more immediate access to the truth, he finds that he is more than ever the helpless subject of "outward things," of the mutable order, and that the truth has grown increasingly dim: "I see the robe now — then I saw the form" (168). Paracelsus' "now" is an instant divested of outer beauty and devoid of inner meaning whereas his "then" was a moment serving as a "wondrous" (160) vesture for the truth within.[14] But he is unable to apply the telling evidence gained from comparing his present with his past state. Instead, the comparison produces more self-pity: "Let me weep / My youth and its brave hopes, all dead and gone / In tears which burn! (189-91). Although admitting to selfish ambitions and addressing God as "mastermind" (229), Paracelsus' primary strategy is to assure the preservation of his own mind. In acknowledging his crime, he perfunctorily repeats the familiar Faustian theme: " ... 'tis thy will, thy righteous will; / I o'erpass life's restrictions, and I die" (233-34). But it is clear that he is merely bargaining, or special-pleading his case, with God, whom he attempts to move first through shame and then through an imperative:

> But if my spirit fail,
> My once proud spirit forsake me at the last,
> Has thou done well by me?   So do not thou!
> Crush not my mind, dear God, though I be crushed!   (238-41)

At this point Aprile enters and finds in Paracelsus his own soul revealed, though the physician's pride will not permit him to gain the like insight through Aprile. Even though Paracelsus has aspired after knowledge and Aprile after love, both share the same fault, which Aprile correctly describes as the desire "to possess at once the full / Enjoyment" by neglecting "all the means / Of realizing even the frailest joy" (389-91). Aprile, too, senses the hostility of the movement of time and wishes to free his "Rare spirit, fettered to a stubborn body" (441) so that he might create a world of his own. But because he regards time as evil, he is helpless to realize his imaginative visions:

> Had we means
> Answering to our mind! But now I seem

> Wrecked on a savage isle: how rear theron
> My palace?   (509-12)

Like Paracelsus, Aprile is frustrated by unyielding dualistic misconceptions; like Pauline's lover, both seek refuge in an isolated, unembodied self.

In accepting this canto as a setting forth of Browning's primary theme, early critics were under the same deception as Paracelsus, who now feels he has only to join love with knowledge to effect humanity's salvation. Certainly Aprile represents no advancement over Paracelsus' own position. He is more strongly aware of his fault and is less given to self-deception, but he, too, is intractably committed to a mistaken course. The reductive lesson Paracelsus draws from Aprile has scarcely taken hold when time again interferes with his idealistic goals, provoking him to identify the object of his hatred: "... I detest all change" (III. 44). As a result of his unyielding pride, Paracelsus still can see only the "robe" and not the "form." He envies Festus, who retains spiritual insight to see "in the stars mere garnishry of heaven, / And in the earth a stage for altars only" (183-84), but can gain no insight from Festus' example. Like Pauline's lover, he has learned nothing from his failure beyond disappointment and self-pity. Frustrated by temporal process, Paracelsus expresses a passionate regret for youth and a longing to be released from time: "I shall rejoice / When my part in the farce is shuffled through, / And the curtain falls" (591-93). Paracelsus' frequent references to acting out a part reflect the fragmentation caused by his dualistic perspective. If his mind is his "true" self, then it must remain imprisoned within the "false," masquerading self of the body. Although Paracelsus could avoid such self-disintegration, he candidly explains why he will not:

> In plain words, I am spoiled; my life still tends
> As first it tended; I am broken and trained
> To my old habits: they are part of me.   (VI. 671-73)

Paracelsus' confession summarizes one of the main themes in Browning's early monodramas — the acquisition of maturity. If the process of adjusting to life's conditions enables the child to become the adult, Paracelsus remains essentially a child because he is a slave to "old habits." Having failed to grow with time, the defenseless spiritual adolescent feels unjustly persecuted by it.

In Canto IV Paracelsus has dropped his self-piteous, defeatist tone to adopt a posture of cynicism and open defiance. His irresponsible, irrational statements suggest the tantrum thrown by a child who has failed to get his way, supporting his characterization of himself as "spoiled." To the horror

33

of Festus, he indicates that he will direct his pursuit to "the meanest earthliest sensualest delight" (244) and that he has no objections to wreaking immediate vengeance upon his foes. But Paracelsus is too intelligent to believe he can so easily compensate for a sense of degradation and, in a moment of sudden candor, assures Festus he has merely been feeding him "childish lies" (326). All he actually desires is a release from time: "This life of mine / Must be lived out and a grave thoroughly earned" (357-58). Closely related to his death wish is a persistent desire to "lapse back into youth" (400), a wish not so much to return to the past as to deny it. Like Pauline's lover and Sordello he would maintain the perspective of youth that has no past and feels quite exempt from time. Failing to recapture youth, Paracelsus is brought back to the realization that, except through death, there is no escape from time. As Canto IV closes, he anxiously counts minutes, caring not "how the farce plays out, / So it be quickly played" (688-89).

Although the time is thirteen years later, there is no indication early in Canto V of any change in Paracelsus' attitude. Delirious and near death, he wavers between contradictory attempts to erase his past and to receive God's approval of it. Failing in both, he reverts to his former cynicism and despair, regarding his life as a waste and blaming "the flagging body" (292) for having "pulled down" (293) the soul. The first sign of a regeneration in Paracelsus comes when Festus recites a quiet, simple lyric depicting a lazily drifting river and the tranquil natural settings through which it flows. The song causes the darkness to flow from Paracelsus' heart and encourages him to use profitably what little time remains in order to tell Festus "God's message" (462). Giving in to the suggestiveness of the flowing river in Festus' song, Paracelsus looks upon life and perceives for the first time "how great the whirl has been" (473). Suddenly everything has lost its former fixity. The gulf rolls and the land "swims past with all its trees, sailing to ocean" (483). As everything yields to the dizzy flux, Paracelsus sees that he is "no less / A partner of its motion and mixed up / With its career" (475-77). The stream image introduced by Festus has become Paracelsus' metaphor for life, and Paracelsus himself is the "good boat" (478) caught up in its current. The mobility in things forces him to examine his consciousness, wherein he discovers the same fluidity:

> Even so my varied life
> Drifts by me; I am young, old, happy, sad,
> Hoping, desponding, acting, taking rest,
> And all at once: that is, those past conditions
> Float back at once on me.   (V. 487-91)

Although the chief source of *Paracelsus*, as DeVane observes in the *Handbook*, was Robert Browning himself, the revelations Browning allows his protagonist often agree with Jung's famous portrait of the sixteenth-century physician. Jung notes the occurrence of a remarkable psychic change in Paracelsus, one manifesting itself as "a transformation of the intellect into a kind of . . . intuitive spirituality." The view of humanity and nature afforded Paracelsus by this event is radically new: "For [Paracelsus] man and world alike are aggregates of animate matter, and this in turn is a notion that has an affinity with the scientific conceptions of the late nineteenth century, except that Paracelsus did not think mechanistically, in terms of inert, chemical matter, but in a primitive animistic way. . . . The animation he experienced psychically was simultaneously the animation of nature."[15]

Going beyond a recognition of the vital, animating principle linking external and internal worlds, Browning's Paracelsus learns that the states of his consciousness not only pass in rapid succession but permeate one another as well. It is foolish, he sees, to separate the past from the present, for consciousness reveals their interpenetration. Whereas fear and resentment had previously driven him to seek an escape from the past, he now is prepared to accept it. Simply by living, man praises God, and the only evidence that he has lived is the totality of his past actions, which he can now examine without shame or disappointment. Thus, in a lengthy and inspired concluding speech, he can justify his unsuccessful pursuit of infinite knowledge as stemming from "Man's inborn uninstructed impulses" (620), which are "august" (619) when their object is to enlighten an ignorant race. From the beginning, Paracelsus had possessed "the secret of the world" (637), an intuition of "what God is, what we are, / What life is" (642-43). He saw that the infinite is not beyond human grasp, for God already

> . . . dwells in all,
> From life's minute beginnings, up at last
> To man — the consummation of this scheme
> Of being . . .   (681-84)

As a result of God's omnipresence, the flux that seems to engulf man represents no threat to him. The disintegration of the earth's surface, the upheavals of the ocean, the activities of the wind — all bear witness to God's immanent presence. The presence of this infinite force within the finite world insures that past and present not only permeate one another but are linked by a creative, evolving power. Thus, man learns that his striving and suffering have value; through his struggling in time he may lay exclusive claim to three hard-won qualities — Power, Knowledge, and Love. Once

35

man's actions in time prove to have immense significance, nature's activities reflect the same vital spirit that is in man. There is never "a senseless gust now man is born" (723), for he has imprinted "for ever / His presence on all lifeless things" (742-43).

William Raymond, who repeatedly emphasized Browning's dual nature as romantic idealist and evolutionary Christian, called the final canto of *Paracelsus* a "Christian representation of love."[16] But surely the conception of love in Paracelsus' dying speech is eclipsed by the boldly original and imaginative presentation of the creative evolutionary process, which has a forward-looking, visionary power that Browning would come back to in the "Epilogue" to *Dramatis Personae*. Indeed, Paracelsus' understanding of the past agrees with that expressed in Bergson's *Creative Evolution*: "Duration is the continuous progress of the past which gnaws into the future and which swells as it advances."[17] In the same book Bergson, in one of the rhapsodic passages that frequently punctuate his work, refers to "the whole of humanity, in space and time," as "one immense army galloping beside and before and behind each of us in an overwhelming charge able to beat down every resistance and clear the most formidable obstacles, perhaps even death."[18] A vision of equal magnitude appears to Paracelsus, for whom the march of time is in step with human progress:

> When all mankind alike is perfected,
> Equal in full-blown powers — then, not till then,
> I say, begins man's general infancy. . . .
> Then shall his long triumphant march begin,
> Thence shall his being date. . . .
> But in completed man begins anew
> A tendency to God.   (750-52, 766-67, 772-73)

Paracelsus is careful, then, to cast no negative implications upon man's quest for the infinite; the pursuit attests to the grandeur of human nature. In defining perfection as imperfection that inspires the endless pursuit of perfection, Paracelsus expresses what would henceforth be a leading idea in all of Browning's poetry. It is definitely misleading to infer that Paraclesus discovers the "great lesson of life": "the finite cannot comprehend the infinite."[19] While he frequently reverts to this medieval Faustian theme as a means of rationalizing his failure or placating God, it hardly represents Browning's final statement. Paracelsus' "naked spirit so majestical" (621) is no more responsible for his failure than is the "intensest life," the "self distinct from all its qualities" responsible for the failure of Pauline's lover. Born with so infinite and glorious a spirit, Paracelsus, in the closing moments of his speech, tries to understand the cause of his failure and finds that growing pride in his power had caused him to reject the very conditions for its expression. He had looked upon the past as valueless and impatiently regarded time as an encumbrance:

> I saw no use in the past: only a scene
> Of degradation, ugliness and tears,
> The record of disgraces best forgotten,
> A sullen page in human chronicles
> Fit to erase. I saw no cause why man
> Should not stand all-sufficient even now.   (812-17)

Only now does Paracelsus realize that he was seriously mistaken to view time as a restriction. As the medium of God's creative energy, time has value in itself; its transfiguring movement permits the evolution of worthwhile goals and the realization of a whole and vital human self.

It is an oversimplification to suggest that Browning attained poetic maturity by repudiating a youthful attraction to Shelley. The spirit of "the Sun-treader," who would effect the freedom of humanity through love, is behind the leading ideas of all Browning's poetry. But Browning had discovered that Promethean ideals need not be punctured by the thorny issues of finite existence. Because love had remained detached from its mundane, temporal origins, Paracelsus and Aprile had failed, but the dying Paracelsus is confident that the examples of Aprile and himself will someday help shape a new and better informed spirit:

> Not so, dear child
> Of after-days, wilt thou reject the past
> Big with deep warnings of the proper tenure
> By which thou hast the earth. . . .
> But thou shalt painfully attain to joy,
> While hope and fear and love shall keep thee man!
>   (826-29, 836-37)

While Canto V is undeniably a powerful expression of some of Browning's deepest convictions, *Paracelsus* is a poem with problems too numerous to allow Browning an artistic triumph. Much of the poem seems painfully repetitious. Paracelsus aspires in Canto I, and in each of the remaining cantos is seen ruminating upon his failure. Even in the final long speech of Canto V he recounts much of what he has already said elsewhere in the poem. The effect of this repetition is that of an event twice reported, since Browning chooses to exclude all dramatic action in favor of tracing its effects upon character. The poem depicts a period of thirty-four years in Paracelsus' life, and although a definite period of time — from two to fourteen years — separates each of the five cantos, Paracelsus' mental and emotional state remains remarkably fixed throughout the poem. Despite Browning's expressed intention of tracing the progress of mood itself, the poem fails to attain a special position in early stream-of-consciousness writing. Paracelsus' lengthy speeches are too set, too carefully deliberated upon to suggest the flow of elemental consciousness. His consciousness appears to be static, occupied more with abstract ideas than with concrete events and spontaneous emotions. The other characterizations, moreover, are far too flimsy to afford much dramatic interest. Festus alternates as a better conscience and a devil's advocate to Paracelsus so that Browning may fully delineate and justify Paracelsus' position. Michal is so incompletely drawn the reader can scarcely recall her when at the close of Canto IV Paracelsus is deeply grieved to learn of her death. Aprile, of course, is a personification of romantic, idealistic love and has little credibility as a character.

In *Paracelsus* Browning brings together his most characteristic thoughts about time to show the tenuousness of human existence when the present lacks duration. In the mature dramatic monologues Browning is able to convert this conviction into poetic practice, taking as his subject not any particular theory about the moment but the moment itself. Thus the moment — the early morning hour during which Fra Lippo Lippi addresses his captors, for example — is made to contain the dramatic action of the poem. As a result, not only does dramatic conflict become more immediate, but dramatic form undergoes enormous compression. As the moment is allowed to expand within the consciousness of the speaker, the boundaries of the original chronological unit are no longer restrictive. Fra Lippo Lippi appears on the stage very briefly, yet the poet is able to evince the substance of an entire lifetime within a limited, measured amount of time. Paradoxically, Browning would not discover the complementary relationship between complex psychological time and compact poetic form until *Sordello*, a poem better known for combining prolixity with incomprehensibility.

III

In *Pauline* and *Paracelsus* Browning had thoroughly immersed himself in the consciousness of his protagonists so that he might reveal the consequences of their impatient attempts to bypass the limitations of a finite existence. By the time of *Sordello* he is able to stand apart from his hero and speak out confidently as master of what has become a familiar theme:

> So, to our business, now — the fate of such
> As find our common nature — overmuch
> Despised because restricted and unfit

38

To bear the burthen they impose on it —
Cling when they would discard it; craving strength
To leap from the allotted world, at length
They do leap, — flounder on without a term,
Each a god's germ, doomed to remain a germ
In unexpanded infancy, unless . . .
But that's the story — dull enough, confess! (III, 975-84)

This passage reveals the similarities of *Sordello* to the previous two poems and implies an important difference as well. Immediately apparent is the opposition of an idealistic temperament to the conditions of a finite and temporal world — an antagonism which, as Pauline's lover and Paracelsus discovered, paradoxically increases the sense of time's hostility. Pauline's lover, who never is able to overcome his consuming egoism, and Paracelsus, who admits that he is "spoiled," both demonstrate that ignorance of time's creative potential dooms one to "remain a germ in unexpanded infancy." But, as the word "unless" indicates, Browning intends to go further in *Sordello* than a mere portrayal of the hero's failure, which is even more conclusive here than in *Pauline* and *Paracelsus*. If Sordello remains a germ, his creator does not. Not only had Browning learned much from the two earlier poems but *Sordello*'s gestation period of seven years would permit him the reflection necessary to achieve a significant breakthrough in his art.

Pauline had been concerned with a poet's struggle to achieve artistic perfection and *Paracelsus* with the efforts of a scientist-reformer to realize his dream for benefiting society. *Sordello* follows the endeavors of a young idealist whose career encompasses both the ivory tower and the market place. The poem makes clear that Sordello's failure first as a poet and secondly as a social reformer stems from the same flaw, which the narrator generously spells out to the reader. Browning must have realized the hazards involved when a poet labors to unburden himself of a heavily didactic message, and he would have had no difficulty in extracting from the perplexed and disbelieving readers of *Sordello* a confession that the poem is "dull enough." But the problem confronting Sordello had preoccupied Browning far too long to be lightly set aside. Torn between sympathy and disdain for the type of character that would once again serve as subject for a long poem, Browning devised a method that would permit at once a close identification with the inner life of his hero and an objective, critical point of view toward the character's shortcomings. The poet's voice is heard not only in his *persona* but in a narrator who comments upon and even participates in the story. The effect is to transfer the main focus of interest from the consciousness of Sordello to that of his creator.

The drawback of this method is that the reader's attention is now divided between the narrative action and the commentary, which need not proceed in the same direction as the story. The passage quoted above, in which the narrator announces his intention to get to the business of the story, occurs almost midway through the poem. Such liberties with chronology are certainly a source of the reader's confusion, which Elizabeth Barrett accurately described: "I think that the principle of association is too subtly in movement throughout *Sordello* — so that *while* you are going straight forward you go at the same time round and round until the progress involved in the motion is lost sight of by the lookers on."[20]

That Browning was aware of the structural as well as linguistic challenges of his narrative is evident when he proposes simply to put the character on stage, "leaving you to say the rest for him" (I. 17). The narrator will provide the raw materials, the disjointed temporal data of human consciousness, but it is the reader's responsibility to discover a significant pattern revealing, as Browning put it in his preface to the 1863 edition, "the development of a soul." The reader's activity, in fact, must be constitutive as well as perceptual. Sordello's method is to station men and women on the platform only to "unstation" (V. 603) them later, a technique he shares with the narrator:

> Man's inmost life shall have yet freer play:
> Once more I cast external things away,
> And natures composite, so decompose
> That . . . Why, he writes *Sordello!* (V. 617-20)

The narrator's reflexive allusion to his poem leaps out at the reader with a sudden, unexpected force. In revealing the complicity of his method and Sordello's, the poet at this late point seems to be taking away even the sparse narrative supports he had originally promised the reader. Like *Sordello*, Browning composes his poem by first decomposing it, then inviting the reader to struggle with him in the task of re-composing, or creating, meaning out of the disparate parts.

The key to structure and technique in Sordello can be found in what Browning later in life confirmed as the major theme of the poem:[21] Sordello's fault of "Thrusting in time eternity's concern" (I. 566). Under this basic conflict a number of other oppositions in the poem can be subsumed, including finite vs. infinite, time vs. space, succession vs. simultaneity, thought vs. perception, meaning vs. form. In no other Browning poem is the dialectic between opposing forces felt more intensely, perhaps because the conflict occurs at the fundamental level of the creative process itself. The opposites mirror the struggle of the poet to separate the narrator from the main character and, in the process, create a unique poetic identity, or self.

40

The first two books of *Sordello* follow a young poet's efforts to make his outer world conform with his Apollonian fantasies. Like the poet in *Pauline*, who had identified himself with Shelley, Sordello's concern is to proclaim and savor his uniqueness. This time, however, it is Browning as narrator who addresses the spirit of Shelley:

> ... stay — thou, spirit, come not near
> Now — not this time desert thy cloudy place
> To scare me, thus employed, with that pure face!   (I. 60-62)

The passage is not simply a conventional apology for undertaking an ambitious project but signals a new objectivity in the poet's handling of character. In *Pauline* the hero's idolatrous attachment to Shelley establishes the latter as the poet's alter ego. Browning tries to preclude this possibility in *Sordello* by establishing the narrator's separate identity before introducing us to the idealistic excesses of his hero.

When Sordello appears, he is in his chamber at Verona, meditating on a certain lady while hectic affairs of state transpire around him. Before continuing with Sordello's actions in the present, however, Browning elects to take the reader back thirty years in order to retrace the development of the poet-child at Goito. This deviation from strict chronological narration marks a new development in Browning's art, as though a more secure grasp of the self's temporal nature demanded of the poet more restless, experimental forms of expression. Elizabeth Barrett's objection that the narrator moves forward and backward at the same time could have made little impression on a poet fascinated by the psychological implications of temporal relationships. In fact, Browning's experiments with time in *Sordello* anticipate Bergson's insistence that "states of consciousness, even when successive, permeate one another and [that] in the simplest of them the whole soul can be reflected."[22] In focusing not on chronological progression or external action but on the development of a soul, Browning could not deal with one stage of a character's life without becoming implicated in all stages. If he were asked to do otherwise, his response would undoubtedly match Sordello's:

> 'Observe a pompion-twine afloat;
> Pluck me one cup from off the castle-moat!
> Along with cup you raise leaf, stalk and root,
> The entire surface of the pool to boot.
> So could I pluck a cup, put in one song
> A single sight, did not my hand, too strong,
> Twitch in the least the root-strings of the whole.
> How should externals satisfy my soul?'   (II. 775-82)

The moment at which Sordello first appears is simply what is visible on the surface, an index to a complicated network of moments comprising the whole. By extending the present moment backward, the poet enables the reader to understand the solitary figure who has just been introduced.

Like Pauline's lover and Paracelsus, Sordello was born into an untroubled, protective environment which allowed him to give free reign to his fancies. The symbol of his seclusion from the outside world is a maple-panelled room and the vault to which it leads. To this inviolate shrine he frequently retires to exercise his imaginative powers upon its marble-maidened font, a recurring image of timelessness and immutability. Not until Sordello emerges from his static and fanciful world can he effectively channel his energies. The narrator comments that Sordello cannot bury himself in something not himself; he is incapable of directing homage outward. Instead, he regards external things as creations of his own soul, laughs at temporal existence and turns inward where his imagination permits him to soar to heaven and be equal to all. The possessor of this latter attitude, the narrator warns, is susceptible to two dangers. He may retreat altogether from "life and time" (I. 557) or, worse, he may attempt to display complete mastery over life and time, "Thrusting in time eternity's concern" (566). This is Sordello's besetting error, and so that its consequences may be seen, the poet returns to his story.

Sordello's protected life at Goito made it difficult for him to break free of the world he had constructed in fancy. Eventually, "time put at length that period to content" (698), and Sordello soon sees that nature, far from bowing before him as its monarch, is quite indifferent to him. But he surrenders none of his self-centered idealism; instead, he continues to feed it by directing his fancies upon an imagined human life rather than upon nature. Soon he has created his own admiring crowd, "stuff / To work his pleasure on" (770). Time does not reveal human beings' actual condition as quickly as it had nature's, and Sordello convinces himself once again that he is Apollo, the unchallenged master of "life and time." Again, however, time attacks the imaginary world of the youth. First, the narrator tells us, "Time stole" (927), and Sordello's fancies are curbed somewhat. Thirty-five lines later, the narrator's comment is more emphatic: "Time fleets: / That's worst!" (962). Sordello realizes that time passes but that he stands still, that he remains an infant. He lacks a real crowd of admirers, and the audience created by his fancy is no longer an adequate consolation.

Finding it increasingly difficult to identify himself with Apollo, Sordello ventures away from Goito and into nearby Mantua, where the celebrated troubador, Eglamor, is winning the approval of the crowd. When Sordello outperforms Eglamor, the crowd rejects the older poet and enthusiastically applauds Sordello, reaffirming his conviction that he "needs must be a god to such" (II. 160). But even while Sordello enjoys his Apollonian fantasies, time whispers sporadic warnings that all is "sure to fade one day" (313). His greatest fear is that he enjoys no essential difference from the common crowd though, like Pauline's lover and Paracelsus, he maintains a stubborn insistence on his uniqueness: " . . . why needs Sordello square his course / By any known example?" (378-79).

If Sordello cannot deny that his body is time's subject, he may still claim a special distinction for his mind. Accordingly, he convinces himself that the separation within him of flesh and a soul which, contrary to flesh, is "averse to change" (II. 401), places him in a position where he may still exact the worship of the common people. Just as Sordello has spurned time, the medium for the realization of his ideals, in his art he also overleaps "means for ends" (491), ignoring "the toilsome process" (489) which enables art to communicate meaningfully. Reluctantly Sordello descends to the temporal universe of thought and language so that his timeless perceptions will be accessible to a human audience:

> Because perceptions whole, like that he sought
> To clothe, reject so pure a work of thought
> As language: thought may take perception's place
> But hardly co-exist in any case,
> Being its mere presentment — of the whole
> By parts, the simultaneous and the sole
> By the successive and the many. Lacks
> The crowd perception? painfully it tacks
> Thought to thought, which Sordello, needing such,
> Has rent perception into: it's to clutch
> And reconstruct — his office to diffuse,
> Destroy.   (II. 589-600)

In this passage Sordello appears to have made the adjustment which would assure his success. He recognizes the dependence of thought on language, which is a pluralistic process communicating meaning only in time. Moreover, he acknowledges the requirement that the poet submit his imaginative vision to deconstruction so that the reader will be permitted to reconstruct its meaning. That his efforts are doomed to failure, however, is implicit in the dichotomy he forces between simultaneous perceptions and successive thought, with the latter being assigned the inferior position. He is still embracing a false view of human experience, a view distorted by "eternal" concerns that continue to be thrust upon time. Not until he dismisses the delusion of expressing a simultaneous truth[23] and celebrates the progressive, unfolding nature of temporal experience can Sordello hope to redeem his life and career. Not surprisingly, his attempt to communicate to the crowd fails, prompting him to rationalize that expression of his "whole dream" to common people would have been an "impertinence" (603).

Pauline's lover and Paracelsus, discouraged after their first encounter with the world of mutability, had attempted to escape to their untroubled youth. Unable to find a vehicle for his philosophical and poetic ideals, Sordello returns to Goito and retires to the timeless solitude of the maple chamber, only to discover that he can no longer be Apollo, since nature and he are "bound by the same bars / Of fate" (III, 92-93). Upon further examination of his comparison between man and nature, Sordello concludes that man definitely has the worst of it. For him there is no regenerative power — "youth once gone is gone" (93) — whereas " 'Nature has time, may mend / Mistake' " (98-99). Eventually Sordello sees that the dynamic principle in nature applies to human beings as well and that happiness belongs to those who " 'Become what they behold; such peace-in-strife, / By transmutation, is the Use of Life . . . ' " (III, 165-66).

Sordello's inability to live what he has learned anticipates a Browning character such as Andrea del Sarto, who also seems powerless to apply his insights. Whereas Andrea's impotence stems from sensual self-indulgence, a complacent resignation to the isolated instant, Sordello's sense of futility arises from his total separation from the temporal order. So accustomed is he to the role of Apollo that he feels singularly exempt from human happiness; there is nothing he may strive to become: " ' . . . what's to blend / With? Nought is Alien in the world — my Will / Owns all already' " (III. 174-76). On an aesthetic level, Sordello's solipsism illustrates the potential trap that awaits the subjective poet, whose preoccupation with his own consciousness eventually leads to a creative impasse by precluding interchange with an external world.[24] On a psychological level, the poet betrays signs of mental imbalance such as those Mill was quick to observe in the poet of *Pauline*. Sordello's condition, in fact, answers to the neurotic state Laing describes in his depiction of the "schizoid" individual. Once reality is located solely in a mental, unembodied self, everything in the outside world, even the subject's own body, is dismissed as inconsequential and unreal. More than anything, the individual at this stage desires to participate in the temporal world yet fears doing so lest his identity be lost.[25] On a spiritual level, Sordello suffers from what Kierkegaard terms "the despair of possibility." As more things become possible, fewer become actual, until the self is swallowed up in its own abyss, unable to escape because of time: "Every little possibility even would require some time to become actuality. But finally the time which should be available for actuality becomes shorter and shorter."[26]

44

For Sordello, the passing of time fills him with anxiety over missing his last opportunity to share in the real life of human beings. Before night falls on his life, he plans somehow to force his imaginative will upon the "pageant time repeats / Never again" (210-11).

The occasion of the anticipated political marriage of Richard and Palma permits Sordello to venture forth once again from Goito and returns the reader to the present moment of Book I when Sordello first appears at Verona. Browning announces that Sordello has completed one round of life and has learned "that a soul, whate'er its might, / Is insufficient to its own delight" (III. 565-66). In order to comment further on the limitations of an isolated, wholly imaginative existence and to suggest a more productive employment of human energies, the narrator shifts to the present tense and to Venice, where he is reflecting upon the composition of *Sordello* and the relationship between poetry and life. Venice with its mixture of good and evil is a symbol of all human activity, and it inspires the poet's conviction that the men most worthy of praise are not idealists like Sordello but men "of action," men like Salinguerra who carry on "the work o' the world" (917, 923). Likewise, the best poet is not one who simply advertises ("the worst of us . . . say they so have seen" 866) or describes ("the better, what it was they saw" 867) his imaginative feats. He ranks with the best only when he is able to "impart the gift of seeing to the rest" (868), impelling others to action. Moreover, if the poet wishes to reach others, he cannot afford to substitute his private dreams of perfection for actual life. Once he is capable of looking squarely at temporal existence and accounting for it all, he will enter the select group of the "Makers-see" (927).

The narrator is thus taking his poet-hero to task for indulging himself in fantasy and producing an ineffectual art. As see-er, Sordello's calling is to impart his gift of seeing to others. But to do so is beyond his power, for like the subjective poet from the *Essay on Shelley*, Sordello is "rather a seer . . . than a fashioner, and what he produces will be less a work than an effluence."[27] From a modern psychological perspective Sordello's inability to act is illuminated by Laing's phenomenological account, as adapted from Hegel: "It can readily be understood why the schizoid individual so abhors action as characterized by Hegel. The act is 'simple, determinate, universal.' But his self wishes to be complex, indeterminate, and unique. The act is always the product of a false self. The act or the deed is never his true reality. He wishes to remain perpetually uncommitted 'to the objective element'."[28]

Following the digression critical of Sordello's isolation and passivity, the narrator returns to Sordello, who finally decides to emulate Salinguerra, the man of action, and align himself with the political power that has the

45

people's best interest at heart. But the poet's examination of Salinguerra's inner consciousness reveals a man entirely different from Sordello. The present moment for Salinguerra extends backward, revealing a continuity of the past with the present. Not only is there dynamic interpenetration of all the moments of his life but a building-up process as well:

> Of such, a series made his life, compressed
> In each, one story serving for the rest —
> How his life-streams rolling arrived at last
> At the barrier, whence, were it once overpast,
> They would emerge, a river to the end . . .   (IV. 452-56)

While Salinguerra's consciousness reveals a purposeful evolution, Sordello, who has existed in a timeless void, is mentally and spiritually stagnant. The difference between the two men is reflected even in their physical appearances. Salinguerra, who is sixty years old and who has always insisted that "life must be lived out in foam and roar" (815), could be mistaken for a youth. Sordello, on the other hand, has done nothing in his thirty years and is "lean, outworn and really old, / A stammering awkward man" (421-22). Yet the actions of Salinguerra have apparently failed to alleviate the suffering of the people. He has the means but lacks the noble vision, while Sordello possesses the vision but can neither realize it for himself or communicate it to others. Still a long way from being a "Maker-see," Sordello determines to save humanity by throwing off the weight of the past and building the new Rome, symbol of the attainment of peace and harmony. In rejecting the past, however, he insures the failure of his dream through ignorance of the temporal conditions essential to the evolution of a new order. The narrator, an ever-present judge and critic of his protagonist, scolds Sordello for "leaping o'er the petty to the prime" (V. 51), for attempting to merge "all epochs in a life time, every task / In one" (61-62).

At first resentful toward time for once more consigning a beautiful vision to the "list of abortions" (V. 72), Sordello begins to awaken to the significance of "the minute's work" (87). He sees that to take the last step first would be to assume God's own prerogative. Man takes one step at a time, and in so doing adds to the great store of the past. Deciding to act upon the first opportunity, however small, to advance humanity's cause, Sordello believes the chance to prove "the past were yet redeemable" (305) lies in helping the Guelfs in their war against the Ghibellines. He will attempt to persuade Salinguerra, military leader of the Ghibellines, to stop fighting and to support the Guelf cause in the best interest of humanity. But Sordello's divided self, his difficulty in finding a verbal medium equal to his deepest feelings, prevents him from communicating with Salinguerra, until the

46

latter's flippant and condescending remarks concerning poets provoke him to renew his efforts at persuasion. This time there is no self-conscious separation of "him who felt from him who spoke" (334), for the spontaineity of his response encourages the emergence of an integrated, embodied self. Through an act of intuition Sordello is able to draw upon his past perceptions and discover their creative potential:

> 'T is Knowledge, whither such perceptions tend;
> They lose themselves in that, means to an end,
> The many old producing some one new,
> A last unlike the first. (V. 443-46)

Replacing enclosed, spatial constructs with dynamic, temporal ones, Sordello now sees the essence of external form is to "extend — / Never contract" (532-33). He was indeed vain to view the outer world as a dim copy of his imagination, for the change and novelty in nature reveal a creative force irreducible to a single mind. In immersing himself in the durational stream of this world, Sordello discovers the proper medium for his creative energy and achieves a new orientation with human existence. The true poet, he sees, differs from other people only in degree. He "has climbed / Step after step" (565-66) ahead of all others and consequently is always at the vanguard in the soul's progress toward freedom. Through song he communicates the vision he has progressively realized to other men who then act upon it. Since "Today / Takes in account the work of Yesterday" (627-28), Sordello is able to renew his hope of a new language — "brother's speech" (635) — which will be capable of embodying and directly communicating whole perceptions. The failure of his earlier attempt was due to his presumptuous detachment from life and time; now he foresees the possible realization of his goal through the evolving power of time.

Salinguerra's proffer of the imperial badge to Sordello immediately threatens his new understanding. The small good he could contribute to the people through awaiting time's result seems insignificant in comparison to the full and immediate power he would enjoy as military leader of the Ghibellines: " 'Speed their Then, but how / This badge would suffer you improve your Now!' " (VI. 319-20). But his sophistry abruptly comes to a halt. The "mere secondary states" (459) created by his intellect are cast aside as he penetrates to "his soul's essence" (460). The "flesh-half's break-up" allows a climactic self-discovery to be "evolved" (466), for "the sudden swell / Of his expanding soul" (467-68) reveals to him that all the states of experience — "Sorrow and Joy, Beauty and Ugliness" (469) — are "modes of Time" (472). Sordello perceives the dynamic reality yet feels powerless to act upon this knowledge. Although he has seen the dangers of an extreme

47

subjectivity, the introspective habit is ultimately too strong to permit him to break free of his mental isolation:

> Once this understood,
> As suddenly he felt himself alone,
> Quite out of Time and this world.... (VI. 484-86)

The narrator's final diagnosis of Sordello's condition recalls the thematic polarity identified early in the poem. In thrusting too much soul on matter, Sordello had overtaxed the body and consequently had found "the minute gone" (520) before he could realize his ambitions. To avoid such disappointment he must learn to

> Fit to the finite his infinity,
> And thus proceed for ever, in degree
> Changed but in kind the same.... (499-501)

Though Sordello has repeatedly given evidence of sharing the narrator's understanding, he finds he cannot modify the demands of his youthful idealism. Time continues to seem unjust and oppressive — a "cloud of hindrance" (555) — when it constantly deprives an exceptional soul of its proper knowledge and joy. Seeing the need to reconcile himself with time, Sordello cannot make the intuitive response which enables one to actually *live* time, to experience temporal flow as duration. In a dilemma over whether he should accept Salinguerra's offer of power or sacrifice himself to the imperceptible advance of the multitude, Sordello dies.

Sordello's death interests the narrator far less than the problematic questions it raises for the artist. As the climax of the poem approaches, the narrator first asks if the body's claims to enjoyment cannot elude the pre-emptive requirements of the soul and then, through poetic troping, suggests a better balance:

> Like yonder breadth of watery heaven, a bay,
> And that sky-space of water, ray for ray
> And star for star, one richness where they mixed
> As this and that wing of an angel, fixed,
> Tumultuary splendours folded in
> To die. (VI. 564-70)

The simile for the relationship of body and soul introduces metaphors — "yonder breadth of watery heaven," "that sky-space of water" — that overturn their own identity as spatial referents. Browning disturbs the pull of the reader's normal cognitive processes by using "watery" and "bay" to describe the sky while "sky-space" refers to the water. In obliterating the familiar outlines of concrete form and intermixing natural scenes with their reflected images, the poet thus achieves the temporalization of space upon which his poetry of duration depends. The violation forced on body by soul and on time by eternity is healed by the dissolving of the intellect's customary distinctions between space and time.

Yet the persistence of the narrator's problem is revealed in the startling decadence of the concluding simile. Here space and eternal stasis are suddenly reinstated as the dynamic interchange of sea and sky gives place to the stable and "fixed" image of an angel. Moreover, the fetishistic dismemberment which enables the angel's two wings to represent body and soul anticipates the fatal discontinuity — "to die" — which closes the conceit. The narrator's first attempt at uncovering an integrated, dynamic self has merely yielded a corpse. Betraying the narrator's dissatisfaction with his own analogy is the adjective "tumultuary" which, when juxtaposed against "fixed," suggests the confused and contradictory nature of this preliminary account of the soul's relation to the body.

The replacement of the original vital metaphor — an act of seeing — with a derivative dead one — a reflexive reaching for the merely decorative — underscores the struggle within the narrator between two ways of knowing. The intuitive approach yields to the intellectual, and temporal sources of knowledge to spatial, when the poet's apprehension of a dynamic self provokes apprehension over its elusiveness. Consequently the narrator returns to the body-soul problem through a question introducing a principle of continuity:

> Never may some soul see All
> — The Great Before and After, and the Small
> Now, yet be saved by this the simplest lore,
> And take the single course prescribed before,
> As the king-bird with ages on his plumes
> Travels to die in his ancestral glooms?
> But where descry the Love that shall select
> That course?   (VI. 579-86)

"To die" echoes the identical infinitive from the preceding simile for the soul's death, but with a difference. Here the finality of dying is challenged not only by the interrogative context but the mythic as well. The "kingbird," or phoenix, "with ages on his plumes" bears only superficial resemblance to the angel's "fixed," folded-in wings, for its "course" is a temporal one forever subject to the possibility of renewal. It lives in time, but time — the ancestral past — also lives in it, making possible a saving regeneration of spirit. Likewise, the self may "yet be saved" when it abandons spatial dis-

49

continuities and follows the unified, dynamically continuous course of duration.

The love required to embark on this course is both transcendent — "a Power above," "utterly incomprehensible" (VI. 591-92) — and immanent — "a Power its representative," "for authority the same" (598-99) that is "revealed" (601) in time. One of Browning's favorite images for this latter, mediate power is the human face. In "Saul" it is a face that humanizes and revitalizes a frozen universe, just as in the "Epilogue" to *Dramatis Personae* "it decomposes but to recompose, / Become my universe that feels and knows" (100-01). In *Sordello*'s climactic passage it is once again a face that enables the narrator to tap the resources of an evolving human power, thereby realizing the potential of the self for creative renewal:

> . . . that face retained
> Its joyous look of love! Suns waxed and waned,
> And still my spirit held an upward flight,
> Spiral on spiral, gyres of life and light
> More and more gorgeous — ever that face there
> The last admitted! (VI. 801-06)

The face, which serves as an inspiration and a perpetual reference point for the ascending spirit, enabling it to measure its progress, belongs to Eglamor,[29] Sordello's poetic inferior. It is significant that just prior to the above passage Browning dismisses Naddo, representing the spirit of critical dissection, and reintroduces Eglamor, the spirit of creative synthesis. Eglamor's limits — his decorous, static, completed forms (III. 617-20) — expose his limitations as a poet. Sordello had simply disposed of his rival, regarding him, like the fixed forms of the past, as an obstacle and challenge to his own creative purposes. The narrator, however, is scrupulously careful to live above rivalry and jealousy (VI. 595-96, 812-13). He brings Eglamor back to life in order to show that the future takes its direction from the past, that the newness of the present moment would be lost without the persistence of the past. Browning prepares to leave his poem by writing the poetry of duration, not pitting singer against singer but celebrating the creative spirit that joins all.

Despite Browning's apparent detachment from the hero, the precise relation of the speaker to Sordello is never altogether clear. It has been suggested that Sordello is but a projection of the speaker, whose conscious and unconscious processes are the real object of inquiry. The speaker's main problem is the same as Sordello's: intellectual reflection prevents him from orienting himself with a world lying outside his self-consciousness. Like Sordello, he tends to disjoin "him who felt from him who spoke" and consequently has as much trouble communicating his message as does Sordello. The problem of comprehension, which has made *Sordello* one of the most notorious and least read poems in the English language, becomes central, then, to the experience the poet intends to convey — that of the self-conscious mind grappling with itself.[30]

This latter explanation is certainly an attractive one for the poem's unyielding obscurities, as the evidence would indicate a close involvement of the speaker with Sordello. Like an overly zealous parent the speaker alternately praises and scolds, encourages and mocks his aberrant child. He so frequently dwells on Sordello's failure — its cause and cure — that he betrays a vital personal interest in the theme. The inclusion of numerous interpretive comments makes it clear, moreover, that the poet, like Sordello, is falling considerably short of his own ideal of the "Maker-see."

Nevertheless, there is a distinction between the narrator and Sordello, one nearly dissolved throughout much of the poem but present all the same. The key to Sordello's difference from the narrator is to be found, once again, in his unshakable need to possess conclusive meaning at once, to force eternity upon time. Sordello's distrust of discursive language and search for a form of language, or "brother's speech," capable of transmitting whole perceptions leave him open to a deconstructionist reading. Derrida attacks the notion that speech possesses a stable, present meaning enabling it to precede and preempt writing. Instead, writing, as Derrida tries to demonstrate, precedes speech, endlessly displacing meaning and placing it beyond the reach of stable, self-authenticating knowledge. Language can never offer total and immediate access to thought for, like time, it involves the endless deferring of presence.[31]

In *Sordello* it is the narrator who acts as deconstructionist critic to the hero's naive insistence on possessing immediate and total truth. An example of the narrator's method can be seen when Sordello, at the beginning of Book V, watches his dream of a new Rome "drop arch by arch" (1. 7). One critic uses this section to support the contention that in *Sordello* Browning practically abandons human rationality if not the English language.[32] While the passage certainly offers problems, they would seem insufficient to contribute to the confusion and notoriety that have denied *Sordello* its share of readers.

Browning's clarifying headnote in the 1863 edition is a question — "Mankind Triumph of a Sudden?" — answered in the text by pointedly ironic questions that mock Sordello's presumptions:

> Art possessed
> Of thy wish now, rewarded for thy quest

51

> To-day among Ferrara's squalid sons?
> Are this and this and this the shining ones
> Meet for the Shining City? Sooth to say,
> Your favoured tenantry pursue their way
> After a fashion! This companion slips
> On the smooth causey, 't'other blinkard trips
> At his mooned sandal. "Leave to lead the brawls
> Here i' the atria?" No, friend! He that sprawls
> On aught but a stibadium . . . what his dues
> Who puts the lustral vase to such an use?   (V. 7-18)

In presenting the drunken, rowdy, crude citizens who populate the "Shining
City" (the reader is left to imagine how the purifying waters of the lustral
vase might be profaned by such types), the narrator allows Sordello's dream
to expose its own limitations. The citizens benefiting from rewards which
they had nowise earned could hardly be expected to appreciate or even comprehend their privileges.

In the next passage, introduced in the 1863 edition by the headnote,
"Why, the Work Should Be One of Ages," Browning offers a correction to
Sordello's plan for building Rome in a day. Here the narrator abandons the
role of deconstructionist critic and creates a montage of events which, despite
considerable temporal complexity, achieve a kind of cinematic coherency:

> Any cave
> Suffices: throw out earth! A loophole? Brave!
> They ask to feel the sun shine, see the grass
> Grow, hear the larks sing? Dead art thou, alas,
> Am I dead! But here's our son excels
> At hurdle-weaving any Scythian, fells
> Oak and devises rafters, dreams and shapes
> His dream into a door-post, just escapes
> The mystery of hinges. Lie we both
> Perdue another age. The goodly growth
> Of brick and stone! Our building-pelt was rough,
> But that descendant's garb suits well enough
> A portico-contriver. Speed the years —
> What's time to us? At last, a city rears
> Itself! nay, enter — what's the grave to us?
> Lo, our forlorn acquaintance carry thus
> The head! Successively sewer, forum, cirque —
> Last age, an aqueduct was counted work,
> But now they tire the artificer upon
> Blank alabaster, black obsidion,
> — Careful, Jove's face be duly fulgurant,
> And mother Venus' kiss-creased nipples pant
> Back into pristine pulpines, ere fixed
> Above the baths.   (V. 23-46)

52

The play of psychological against chronological time is seen in the narrator's self-reflexive references — "Dead art thou, alas, / And I am dead!," "Lie we both / Perdue another age," "What's time to us? . . . what's the grave to us?" — which act as cinematic "cuts" in a minipageant of human history evolving from cave dwellers to artificers of the most refined, sensual sculpture. The poet need not be dismayed by the sluggish progress of primitive artisans whose pedestrian dreams fail to comprehend the mystery of door hinges. In declaring the narrator and hero "dead" rather than unborn, Browning places the poet in relation to a dynamic process rather than a temporal continuum, which Bergson would call a mere spatialized representation of the experience of time. The poet's role is reversed from that of descendant to progenitor precisely because Browning wants to upset the reader's expectations of chronological sequence and force reconsideration of that role. The poet is neither fabricator of utopian wholes nor a mere stage in the development of such projects. His task is to embody the perceptions of a dynamic self in a poetry revealing the temporal values of human existence, a poetry of duration that refuses to mourn the ravages of time — "that scurvy dumb show" — but insists instead on rejoicing in the magnificent procession — "this pageant sheen" (48).

If *Sordello* itself does not offer the reader an orderly procession, its circuitous route is the only effectual one Browning could have taken. The digressions and discontinuities within the poem's narrative structure serve to mirror the consequences of Sordello's violations upon time as well as to dismantle the efforts themselves. In the process, Browning is submitting to the humbling, terrifying ordeal of unmaking his own poetic identity so that when he finally dismisses Sordello — "thus bereft / Sleep and forget, Sordello!" (VI. 870-71) — he may confront his readers — "friends, Wake up!" (873-74) — with a remade, revitalized self. With the gratuitous but emphatic announcement that only those who choose may hear Sordello's story (I.1, VI. 886), Browning suggests that the reader's role in the text is secondary to the composer's.[33] The poem is, after all, not so much Sordello's story as the narrator's, whose immersion in the shifting streams of his own consciousness is Browning's equivalent for the ritualistic underworld descent that precedes creative rebirth. The cost of this experimentation is the disjointed associationism that Miss Barrett disapproved of and that Bergson would likely decry for replacing the continuity of becoming with a discontinuous multiplicity of elements.[34]

Yet *Sordello*, especially in its handling of time and place, shows Browning's growing mastery of poetic form. Whereas the objective setting of *Paracelsus* contributed practically nothing to dramatic effect or to a sense of immediacy, in *Sordello* it provides both a unifying link for the digressions and a sense of urgency to the little that Sordello does. From Sordello's appearance at Verona in Book I to his death at Ferrara in Book VI the actual chronology is no more than two days. Meanwhile, through the recurring references to Goito and to the conflict between Guelfs and Ghibellines, the poet is able to extend backwards some thirty years in Sordello's life and several hundred years in Italian history. Consequently, Salinguerra's offer of the imperial badge to Sordello becomes acutely significant because of the reader's awareness of its relation to the past.

In *Sordello* — contrary to *Pauline* and *Paracelsus* — Browning presents a climactic, or critical moment, which at once expresses and judges the life-content of the person experiencing it. Despite its bulk and inefficiency *Sordello* anticipates not only the temporal problems Browning would address in the plays but the compression he would eventually achieve with the dramatic monologue form.

IV

After Browning's efforts — not entirely successful — to dissociate himself from his hero in *Sordello*, the next step away from the confessional form of *Pauline* was the drama, which Browning undoubtedly felt would provide the objectivity necessary to make him readable to the public. The thematic concern of the plays echoes a problem Browning investigates throughout his poetry — the ability or inability to act. After *Sordello*, Browning's characters no longer suffer from adolescent illusions of omnipotence. Their problem may be stated as the progressive realization of self through free and spontaneous actions that penetrate custom and convention, as well as all restrictive forms of the dogmatic mind. The problem of inaction, then, is no mere structural deficiency but is central to the dramatic conflict which is presented in each play. A continual battle between heart and head is waged within and occasionally among characters who search for an action that will express their fullest and deepest selves.

Browning in the plays, however, has not modified his concerns to fit the requirements of the theater. His interest is still focused on the mental life of a character whose psychological problems are too intricate to be revealed through mere suggestion. Consequently, the external elements of the play tend to accompany rather than reveal character and the character rarely seems to act in a significant manner. Browning was fully aware of this effect in his first play, *Strafford*, which he described as "one of Action in Character, rather than Character in Action."[85] But it is unlikely that he understood

54

the full implication of his approach. Once action is located within the character, the action which takes place outside — including setting and circumstances of the plot — is in danger of becoming superfluous. It merely confuses and annoys the viewer while diverting attention from the internal conflict the author wishes to emphasize.

An equally damning weakness of the plays is Browning's failure to provide the illusion that the characters have independent lives of their own. With protagonists such as Djabal, Luria, Chiappino and Tresham, a strongly felt point of view seems to be in control from the outset. Whereas forceful drama derives much of its vitality from an eruptive, spontaneous clashing of partially understood motives, Browning in most of his plays is simply incapable of suspending judgment. The role-playing at which he is so adept in the dramatic monologues is strangely reversed in the plays, where characters serve as unconvincing representatives for the poet's ideas. It is apparent that what Browning required was an internal stage, where he would have room to explore and develop the numerous currents in a single character's mind, allowing the character to reveal his own inconsistencies. In addition, he needed a structure that would require him to compress the entire lifetime of the character within a single dramatic situation.

Browning's plays cannot be dismissed without some consideration of *Pippa Passes*, perhaps the only play by Browning which attracts the notice of the general reader today. Written immediately after *Sordello*, *Pippa Passes* may be seen as a reaction against the intellectual obscurities and arcane language of the earlier poem. The heroine is certainly a striking contrast for Browning. An innocent silk-weaver who unconsciously affects others with her simplistic lyrics, Pippa is totally unreflective of her relation to the outside world in which she exists as a passive agent. Thomas Collins has suggested that the play represents "a retreat from poetic responsibility." Through a hard-won struggle in *Sordello* Browning had succeeded in providing tentative answers to crucial and inescapable questions concerning the artist's relation to humanity. Pippa, however, is "a regression," in Collins' words, "to the uncomplicated vision of youth, the chastened and purified romantic version of a poet who can do all things for all men and yet never become really involved with them."[36] But if Pippa is in some ways an impossible character, her importance as an operative symbol for the poet may be seen as outweighing any consideration of her credibility. The one small backward step Browning committed with the creation of Pippa is almost negligible in comparison to the gigantic leap forward he makes elsewhere in the poem.

If the undramatic nature of Browning's plays stems in large part from the poet's inability to suspend judgment, Pippa emerges as a notable exception, for she is a poet-figure who uses her imaginative gifts solely for identifying with other points of view. Through her Browning endorses the quality of negative capability which, as W. David Shaw suggests in his discussion of the poem, is "the source of the poet's power."[37] Pippa, of course, is totally oblivious to her powers, though at the poem's conclusion she fumbles for a rudimentary defense of poetry:

> Now, one thing I should like to really know:
> How near I ever might approach all these
> I only fancied being, this long day:
> — Approach, I mean, so as to touch them, so
> As to . . . in some way . . . move them — if you please . . .
> (IV. ii. 99-103)

In contrast to Sordello, who articulates a definitive theory of poetics which he is powerless to implement, Pippa actually realizes the role of "maker-see," whose revelations move others to action. She does not resemble Sordello so much as his sole legacy — a youthful and fanciful, fragmentary lyric known only to an innocent child. In *Pippa Passes* Browning furthers the dissociation of poet and poem by adopting this simple child and allowing it to speak for him. Pippa's innocence establishes the poem as protagonist and enables Browning to compose a drama in which the play is, indeed, the thing. The results are immediately and impressively apparent in the tense emotional exchange between Sebald and Ottima, a scene which owes its power to the differences between the characters' problematic relationship with each other and the poet's respectful distance from both. More than revealing the poet's empathy, however, the scene demonstrates the artist's ability to share with others his own capacity for intellectual sympathy. Though Pippa is unconscious of a persuasive end, her songs liberate characters by permitting them to share other points of view.

Liberation may sound like a contradiction in reference to characters whose task is to recognize, in Pippa's words, that "God's puppets, best and worst, / Are we; there is no last nor first" (Introduction, 194-95). The ready submission of the characters to Pippa's song, moreover, has provoked caustic criticism of Browning not only for his creation of Pippa but for characters who emulate her simplicity.[38] Yet in the context of the play these are no ordinary mannequins but paradoxical puppets whose response to the moment frees their torpid wills. If they regress, it is from Sartre to Kierkegaard, from individuals enslaved by their own freedom to spiritual beings momentarily moved by the invisible strings of an infinite relationship. Like the protagonists of Browning's other plays, each of the main characters is challenged to make a significant self-discovery through an appropriate action.

Sebald may yield to Ottima's eroticism or recognize and reject her depravity. Jules may deify and worship Phene from afar or love her as a human being. The choice for Luigi is between remaining at home in the protective custody of his mother or undertaking a hazardous patriotic venture. The Monsignior must decide whether to give tacit approval to a crime advantageous to himself or to intercede before the wrong has been done. In each instance the character experiences a critical moment at which he may passively yield to circumstances inviting spiritual and moral paralysis, or follow his deep convictions and act to alter circumstances.

Of course, Browning's infinite is no remote, transcendent being but an immanent, animate force, the same dynamic power that Paracelsus found at work in nature. Pippa's opening description is of a day charged with energy, beginning with a dawn that moves "Faster and more fast" until it boils, then spurts and, finally, overflows the world (Introduction, 2-12). All's right with this world not because God's in his heaven but because his "Paradise" is always of the world, "his presence fills / Our earth" (Introduction, 192-93). Pippa is an embryonic version of Browning's Pope in *The Ring and the Book*. Although she does not judge the characters, her song serves as the standard by which the characters judge themselves. Just as temporal continuity enables the Pope to feel confident in evaluating a soul by its last act, Pippa views human life as "one deed / Power shall fall short in or exceed!" (Introduction, 200-01). Moreover, the deed that carries something extra, that is capable of redeeming an entire lifetime, can — as Caponsacchi, the Pope's "athlete on the instant," discovered — occur like a flash. The characters exposed to Pippa, who makes much of not squandering or letting slip by a single moment (Introduction, 13, 72), seize at the opportunity for instantaneous salvation. Sebald sees that his murder of Luca is but a metaphoric counterpart to his infatuation with Ottima. He had loved not a total human being but fixated upon hair, neck, breasts, and "faultless shoulder-blades" (I. i. 255). Following such fetishistic dismemberment, Ottima has not surprisingly become empty and lifeless (I. i. 239-47) for Sebald, who now wishes he could return each anatomical part: "Ottima, / I would give your neck, each splendid shoulder, both those breasts of yours, / That this were undone!" (I. i. 124-26). Although Sebald sees his object of desire grotesquely transformed into an object of bitter hatred (I. i. 237, 269), Ottima is released by Pippa's song to a more integrated, spiritual view of their love: "Lean on my breast — not as a breast" (I. i. 274). She has the self-awareness to know, as Pompilia does, that nothing in temporal experience can ever be undone.

57

Jules has reduced Phene not to a sexual object but to an art object removed from temporal process. By identifying himself with the object, he hopes to take on its permanence: "Nay, look over / This one way till I change; grow you — I could / Change into you, beloved!" (II. i. 8-10). Change, from Jules' self-deluded perspective, is equated with stasis. Sitting side by side, and holding hands with Phene, Jules prefigures the image of Andrea del Sarto seeking comfort in a static, enclosed moment with his Lucrezia. The debasement both artists practice before their models recalls the attempts of Pauline's lover to secure comfort by leaning on Pauline, Shelley, and even Andromeda, the changeless figure of a painting. Pippa's song, however, transforms Phene into a human Andromeda, and Jules from posturing servant to autonomous agent:

> If whoever loves
> Must be, in some sort, god or worshipper,
> The blessing or the blest one, queen or page,
> Why should we always choose the page's part?
> Here is a woman with utter need of me, —
> I find myself queen here, it seems!   (II. i. 282-87)

The dynamic, immanent power which Pippa represents frees Jules to discover a new and living soul in a body that had previously existed for him as a blank and passive aesthetic object (II. 288-300).

Similarly, each of the other characters, by abandoning immobilizing rationalizations and submitting to temporal flow, experiences a regeneration of spirit on this New Year's Day. At the same time, the frequent charge that Browning, in Pippa, introduces an intellectually regressive, "born-again" theology is simply insupportable. Though the apocalyptic moment converts each character to a course of action, the reader has no basis for judging salvation complete, for Browning, as usual, refuses to foreclose meaning and to permit a simplified reading of each story. Sebald, Ottima, Luigi and the Monsignior are pried loose from their moral inertia only to confront a world in which change represents imminent death. Jules may start afresh with Phene in some idyllic "isle in far-off seas" (II. i. 319), yet his newly discovered love for a living person will most certainly be tested, as Pippa herself, in referring to Jules' marriage, makes clear: "Lovers grow cold, men learn to hate their wives" (Introduction, 164). Even Pippa's return to her chamber at the close of day resists a decorous closure. She is reminded of her return to the silk mills in the morning, a thought that forces her to question the use to which she has put her single holiday. Just as Pippa cannot know whether her hymn has had the desired effect (IV. ii. 99-110),

Browning seems to be questioning the value of his own poem, deferring the question to the reader's judgment.

Readers of Browning's plays have traditionally judged *Pippa Passes* the best, and the present-day reader is likely to continue to find the characters of this play the most compelling and alive. With the creation of Pippa, Browning handed over the strings to a far less intrusive, less tyrannous puppetmaster. Not only does her song free the characters from their limited perspectives but its natural simplicity encourages them to discover their own feelings as a guideline for action. Roma King sees Pippa functioning as "a primitive anti-intellectual force" that "cuts through sophisticated rationalization" and "encourages action on a basic level."[39] She saves the characters from a static world created by intellect and permits them to awaken to a temporal universe corresponding to the dynamic course of their deepest emotions.

Pippa Passes enjoys other features, of course, that distinguish it among Browning's plays. The action, for instance, is confined to a single day, a compression anticipating the compact time scheme of the dramatic monologue form. The setting is drawn from the poet's impressions of his favorite Italian town and has a vividness that does not reappear in Browning's poetry until he once again portrays Italian natural beauty in "An Englishman in Italy." Moreover, the setting in *Pippa Passes* is no distant backdrop but is an integral element in Browning's characterizations. Like Pippa's song it serves as a commentary on "unnatural" motives and points of view. Despite an implausible heroine and a loose, episodic structure, *Pippa Passes*, far from being a regression in Browning's poetic development, is as instrumental as *Sordello* in pointing the way to the dramatic monologues.

Browning's failure in writing for the stage will always provoke discussion among those familiar with the dramatic qualities of his verse. His deficiencies cannot be traced simply to technical shortcomings but seem to hinge on questions of temperament and aptitude. A mind like Browning's, viewing existence as temporal and dynamic, perceiving reality as constant flux, must find the life of the mind a more congenial subject for dramatic presentation than the external world. Accordingly, Browning's most convincing settings are those derived from the minds of his characters. When he attempts to create external environment first and character second, the results are less satisfying. The esoteric historical settings of most of Browning's plays, for example, strike the modern reader as unnecessarily detailed and obscure. Though Browning in the plays uses the past both as a point of view and a past reflect the immediacy and relevance of those concerns. In the dramatic disguise for examining the present concerns of the self, he fails to make the past reflect the immediacy and relevance of those concerns. In the dramatic monologues he is able to put all action, including setting, in character. Conventional chronology, in turn, is subordinated to a more realistic psychological time in which all of the past is suggested by a present moment which itself becomes the central action as well as the shaping form of the poem.

CHAPTER III

The Specious Present:
The Dramatic Monologue

In *Pauline, Paracelsus,* and *Sordello* Browning portrays characters whose problem is to resist enclosure by the moment. Masterful evaders who choose to run against rather than with time, the protagonists of all three poems experience paralyzing, self-destructive isolation once the moment is reduced to a knife-edge present. A similar thematic perspective shapes Browning's first published dramatic monologues, "Johannes Agricola in Meditation" and "Porphyria's Lover" (1836), poems in which the characters' distorted views of life are indicated by their respective attitudes toward time.

Johannes is a religious fanatic who chooses to believe himself one of God's elect and specially exempt, therefore, from time and change:

> Ere suns and moons could wax and wane,
> Ere stars were thundergirt, or piled
> The heavens, God thought on me his child.... (13-15)

Time is irrelevant to all other men as well, for God has already determined their future:

> Priest, doctor, hermit, monk grown white
> With prayer, the broken-hearted nun,
> The martyr, the wan acolyte,
> The incense-swinging child — undone
> Before God fashioned star or sun! (51-55)

Johannes' dynamic verb choices for God's fashioning of the cosmos cannot hide the static quality of a God-man relationship ordained in pre-temporal thought. His egomaniacal detachment from life, accompanied by his extreme complacency and condescension, makes him a repulsive character despite the compelling lyricism of his argument.

In "Porphyria's Lover" the speaker, contrary to Johannes Agricola, is all too conscious of the effects of time and change. The woman he loves is incapable of returning the lasting affection he desires. For one moment, however, she belongs to him:

> That moment she was mine, mine, fair,
>   Perfectly pure and good.... (36-37)

Confident that Porphyria worships him for this brief instant, the speaker strangles her. His solution to the threatening movement of time is simply to halt its advance by attempting to isolate and preserve a single moment.

Once Browning fully understood the temporal implications of the self's development he began to discover creative uses for time in his portraits of men and women. The concept of a knife-edge present was replaced by the psychological fact of a "specious present,"[1] a moment which partakes of durational flux and extends into both past and future. Although the present moment seems to agree with the bare instant marked by the clock, in the reality of the spiritual life it exists not as an instantaneous point but as an integral part of a continuous and evolving stream of experience. For the poet of the mature dramatic monologues there is nothing terrifying about the fragility of the moment. Browning's concern rather is to enlarge and expand it with significant content — with an elasticity best understood in terms of Bergsonian "duration." Since temporal flow is an accumulative process, manifesting a dynamic continuity of past with present, it is possible to use the moment as an index to an entire lifetime. Browning may call a monstrous poem one "moment's flashing"[2] because that moment is a microcosm of life; implicit within it is the whole of experience.

In addition, the moment functions as a test to character. It is critical to the speakers of Browning's monologues because of his underlying conviction that a human being is "named and known by that moment's feat."[3] The spiritual development that everywhere characterizes Browning's poetic message and receives its most explicit statement in "Rabbi Ben Ezra" is possible only when the individual regards the moment as the opportunity for creative action and growth. The choice is between enslaving oneself to the static world of the intellect or heeding intuition and immersing oneself in the durational stream of the living, dynamic world. The outcome of this struggle between the intuitive self and the illusions of the intellect determines whether or not the crucial moment takes on the quality of duration. When the choice is made by intuition, the "critical minute" becomes the "good minute," the present moment acquires duration.

In the dramatic monologues the moment, then, has two important functions. First, it frequently provides direct thematic interest. The character's response to it is a source of the poem's drama for the reader. Second, it constitutes the action of the poem. The poem in itself *is* a moment representing one characteristic episode of the subject's life. In other words, the moment is *unusual* in that it serves as an epiphany, challenging the speaker to make an important self-discovery, but it is also *characteristic* in that it reflects the whole life of the person experiencing it. Browning's task, then, is to fashion the past so that it is felt as a totality in the present. The methods employed to suggest this dynamic interpenetration of past and present in a self-in-process are diverse and complex, though common to all is the avoidance of closure. The moment depicted by the dramatic monologue must not appear isolated or self-contained, for its ability to suggest a time depth in excess of the form containing it depends on a sense of incompleteness. For this reason, the limits of the monologue are determined in an arbitrary manner; abrupt openings and closings imply discontinuity within the formal structure in order to suggest continuity with moments outside the poem. To insure that both ends of the poem remain open, Browning shuns an orderly beginning and ending as well as rigid narrative chronology because they would suggest completeness, or finality.

The uniqueness of the moment — the quality that makes it "unusual" — is not always apparent from the dramatic situation given in the poem. Though the speaker's moment is often termed "critical," it is frequently not even clear what motivates the speaking, except that the monologist usually feels something can be gained by an unburdening of oneself at this particular instant. The urgency of the situation, then, derives more from the deep emotional concerns of the speaker than from external circumstances. In monologues such as "Andrea del Sarto," "My Last Duchess" and "Cleon" the speaker experiences inner disturbances which he attempts to remove through verbalization. By making a troublesome feeling intelligible to the intellect, the speaker affords to the sensation a fixity accessible to rational control. But at the same time the potential value of the sensation is negated, for it may have directed attention to the stream of consciousness which is the living, authentic self. Rather than examine the experience as it actually feels, the speaker chooses to adapt it to existing concepts of self. Consequently the speaker's experience remains bound to the static structures of the past, and he or she can neither feel nor act in the present moment. The reader's awareness of the discrepancy between the dynamic moment of actual experiencing and the fixed past moment which the speaker attempts to impose on it helps account for the aesthetic tension which is the distinguishing feature of Browning's dramatic monologues. In *The Ring and the Book* Browning even sets this same struggle within the reader, whose own consciousness becomes a subject for examination. Not until the dynamic potential of the immediate moment is realized can the reader come alive to the facts which enable participation in the poem.

The presence of an auditor frequently provides the speaker with the occasion for establishing a defense. Because the speaker is not fully in touch with personal feelings and would more often rather suppress than understand them, the soliloquy form would not serve the speaker's need for self-justification. An auditor's presence, on the other hand, represents a public endorsement of the speaker's rationalizations, thus providing protection from further discomforting sensations and preserving a fabricated self-image. The cleric of "The Bishop Orders His Tomb" illustrates pointedly this relationship between speaker and auditor. As long as the Bishop can imagine that he has his sons' attention, he may rest secure in his fabrications, but when it becomes apparent that his sons ignore him his defenses collapse.

Most of the auditors in Browning's dramatic monologues present no challenge to the speaker, who consequently feels no need to abandon the self's defenses. Occasionally they will cause the speaker to reveal more about self than he obviously intended, but rarely are they responsible for any self-revelation on the speaker's part. They either lack the speaker's intellectual gifts and verbal powers or are inferior in rank. Undoubtedly the speaker has elected to address the audience in the first place because it seems to offer no threat to an existing self-concept. As a result the speaker remains trapped by his rationalizations in a static world crystallized from past experience. Within the enclosed temporal worlds of Andrea del Sarto or the Duke of "My Last Duchess," for example, no progress is made; the "good minute" is never realized.

In a few monologues the speaker is able to respond to the actual flow of experience in the immediate moment. For Fra Lippo Lippi and the speaker of "By the Fireside" the channels of communication between self and experience are unobstructed; each lives fully in the present moment even as it changes. Self is no longer a completed state but a ceaseless process of becoming in which nothing is fixed.[4] For Browning life is at its best, as the speaker of "By the Fireside" discovers, when two people join selves in a moment that is filled with the past yet moves in a forward direction which appears endlessly new.

Finally, the moment of Browning's dramatic monologues, besides deriving importance from the emotional concerns of the speaker, has significance because of the historical situation it reflects. Present in any moment of an individual's life are not only the totality of personal experience but the cultural factors that have helped shape that experience. Browning peers not simply into the life of a single character but into the period of time which the character reflects. Cleon, Andrea del Sarto, and Guido are highly individualized portraits that nevertheless illustrate defects common to the historical period of each. By placing individual problems within a large, universal context Browning expands his thematic scope: whole societies can go wrong when the present is reduced to a durationless point sanctioning moral complacency and greed. Some knowledge of a character's environmental conditioning, moreover, is useful in illuminating the speaker's thoughts and actions. On the other hand, certain characters — Fra Lippo Lippi, Caponsacchi, Childe Roland — have evolved by viewing their environment as an obstacle or challenge rather than a mold. Each chooses to defy rather than submit to the forces that would circumscribe him. Through each, Browning returns to the drama that interests him most: the development of a soul.

I

The Moment Recognized: Monologues on Religion

For Browning the supreme moment of revelation occurs when Christ is recognized as the manifestation of Divine Love. The Incarnation has a central role in Browning's poetry because Jesus, as the culmination of the creative life-process, illuminates the place of the dynamic and spiritual in daily human existence. At each moment of living, the initial revelatory encounter is repeated, a constant challenge to put an end to the old and begin the new: intellectual pride must be overcome by an unassuming, humanistic love; the outworn myth and mechanical ritual of the old religion must be replaced by the creative energy of the new, the spring of life of which is the loving Creator.

Browning conceives of the Incarnation in dynamic and evolutionary terms as a reaction against the rational approaches of his contemporaries. "Bishop Bougram's Apology," though primarily a *tour de force* in rhetorical strategy and characterization, is also a defense of Christianity on pragmatic grounds. When Blougram reads his own soul directly, he reveals that the significance of God's loving act is that it defines faith itself as an act — an endless process rather than a rational state:

> It is the idea, the feeling and the love,
> God means mankind should strive for and show forth
> Whatever be the process to that end, —
> And not historic knowledge, logic sound,
> And metaphysical acumen, sure! (621-25)

Blougram dismisses history and logic for their tendency to fix in the past meaning that is still unfolding in the present. In "A Death in the Desert"

65

the apostle John, the last creature to see Christ with his own eyes, uses the Incarnation to counteract the view of the universe as a purposeless mechanism and to explain man's ability to grow. Since God's revelation through Christ is unceasing, growth is possible when "Man apprehends Him newly at each stage" (432).

The chief difficulty Browning's characters have in recognizing the Incarnation as the self-revealing act of God is their tendency to submit all empirical evidence to the analytical work of the intellect. The dynamic, present-tense character of the Incarnation is itself evidence that God cannot be apprehended by thought but must be sought after and held through action. God's transforming love must be realized through the activity of the whole person; where it is sought in a static past through rational modes it appears not to exist. These opposing responses are presented as an intense struggle within the speakers of the two epistolary monologues, "An Epistle" and "Cleon," poems in which Browning's mastery of psychological drama is unequaled.

In the former poem, Karshish, an Arab physician with a scientifically trained, skeptically curious mind, has met the resurrected Lazarus on his travels and must now submit an irrational experience to his own reason as well as that of his learned teacher. He tries to report the incident with professional objectivity, bringing it up simply as an afterthought in a routine account of his medical experiences, but his awestruck emotions soon force him to disclose the degree of his preoccupation. Making it especially difficult for him to contain his enthusiasm is his wonderment not at the death-to-life feat itself but at the living example of Lazarus, whose quality of life is inaccessible to scientific analysis:

> The spiritual life around the earthly life:
> The law of that is known to him as this,
> His heart and brain move there, his feet stay here.   (183-85)

Karshish's instincts tell him that in Lazarus he has encountered a temporal being who has surmounted the threat of time. Though the speaker fluctuates between skepticism and belief even in the final lines of the poem, the faint tones of denial, retained to satisfy the auditor, are barely heard amid ecstatic exclamations of visionary acceptance. In reporting the words Lazarus had attributed to "The very God" (304), Karshish discloses the self-revaluation that has led him to the edge of conversion. As with the revelatory encounters of David in "Saul" and of the poet in "Epilogue" to *Dramatis Personae*, it is a "Face" wherein are revealed the power and love of God, the knowledge of which comes only through the act of loving:

'Thou hast no power nor mayst conceive of mine,
But love I gave thee, with myself to love,
And thou must love me who have died for thee!'   (309-11)

Whereas "An Epistle" shows time losing its threatening aspect, "Cleon" portrays to a greater degree than any other Browning poem, the intense frustration and horror that the passing of time can hold for an individual. The theme expressed by Browning's Greek poet-philosopher is a familiar one — the problem, once again, of fitting the infinite to the finite:

> ... life's inadequate to joy,
> As the soul sees joy ...
> And so a man can see but a man's joy
> While he sees God's ...   (249-50, 261-62)

In this case, Browning's favorite theme takes on added poignancy, for it is expressed not by a youthful idealist, such as the *Pauline* poet or Sordello, disappointed over his failure to secure the fame and power he desires. Cleon has achieved almost total success in all the arts and is venerated for his wisdom as well as his accomplishments. He clearly enjoys an eminence from which he might be expected to draw, at the very least, enormous personal consolation. Yet he takes little satisfaction in his achievements, regarding them as the inevitable outcome of Greek progress. As a latter day product of this intellectual advancement, Cleon is still very much a loyal spokesman for the Greek way of life. At the same time he cannot conceal an Arnold-like envy of the "simple way" (66) of his forerunners, and he falters in proclaiming his way superior to that of "some whole man of the heroic age" (70).

Cleon's dissatisfaction is not surprising in view of his characteristically Greek view of progress. The Greek frame of mind was one which sought out permanent objects the knowledge of which could be demonstrated rather than processes which could not be intellectually grasped or proven. Because the world of change was less than real it was not considered an object of genuine knowledge.[5] It is surprising, therefore, when H. B. Charlton writes that Cleon sees progress as "a process of evolution, and therefore he finds it an *élan vital* towards perfection or completion."[6] This is the view ultimately expressed by Browning's Paracelsus, but there is no evidence of it in Cleon. Progress for him excludes any principle of growth or change. It consists simply of a mechanical assembly of component parts, each of which has been perfected by Greek know-how at some stage in the past:

> So, first the separate forms were made,
> The portions of mankind; and after, so

67

Occurred the combination of the same.
For where has been a progress, otherwise?
Mankind, made up of all the single men, —
In such a synthesis the labour ends.   (89-94)

Such a view, as Cleon well knows, precludes progress. Since men of the past have already reached the outside boundary of the intellectual faculty and made of all their individual accomplishments a final synthesis, Cleon senses that all he may do is ape their efforts:

Now mark me! those divine men of old time
Have reached, thou sayest, well, each at one point
The outside verge that rounds our faculty;
And where they reached, who can do more than reach?   (95-98)

Exasperated by the prospect of a static, meaningless existence, Cleon turns to Zeus and asks a pointed question: "Why stay we on earth unless to grow?" (114). Cleon himself provides a tentative answer by imagining Zeus as an immanent presence, the "latent everywhere" (126), and thus capable of showing "simultaneously / What, in its nature, never can be shown, / Piecemeal or in succession" (117-19). Since human intellect is powerless to account for change, the superior, supernatural intelligence Cleon imagines as descending to this mutable world has an unmistakably spatial character, not wholly unlike an Olympian deity. But Cleon's logical mind proves unreceptive even to this idea, which he discards as a "fiction" or "dream" (115, 127).

Still looking for an answer to his question, Cleon turns from dream to what he considers real: the progress manifest in nature. Nature's "unwaning powers" (129) contrast so sharply with man's exhausted potential, however, that Cleon finds only a deeper despair and poses a second, more disturbing question: "What, and the soul alone deteriorates?" (138). This is Cleon's first reference to time, which now assumes a strictly villainous role. It had no place in his concept of progress, since even the improvement nature seems to show with each succeeding year is possible only "through culture" (131), that is, through human ingenuity and not through any power apart from man's brain. At this point, then, hostile time is set against Cleon's intellect in an intensifying struggle that constitutes the main action of the poem.

Cleon's first impulse is to compare his creative intellect with knowledge which only the gods possess, and on this basis claim exemption from time (139-55). But the parallel provides no solace. Contrary to the belief of Protus, the king to whom Cleon is writing, superior knowledge does not reduce for Cleon the fear of death, nor does he derive comfort from knowing his works will withstand time. Instead he finds that the development of man's intellectual faculty only increases his unhappiness:

> 'Let progress end at once ... '
> In man there's failure, only since he left
> The lower and inconscious forms of life.   (222, 225-26)[7]

The more man advances in self-consciousness, the more acute is his frustration over the movement of time. In Browning's poetry the realization of self takes time. Cleon, however, sees time as taking the self, leaving only the artist's works behind.

At this point the warring elements in Cleon — pride in man's intellectual "progress" and an intuitive need for meaningful fulfillment in time — are at extreme poles from one another, and he is forced to admit that "Most progress is most failure" (272). As an artist Cleon suggests that his frustration is more acute than that of most men. Since he possesses the imaginative gifts to know and show the joys of living, his inability to experience such joys for himself is doubly exasperating. He sees that even his fair she-slave is more attracted to a muscular rower than to himself, "grown too gray / For being beloved" (297-98). The art which Cleon mastered after years of painful struggle seems a costly acquisition now. That which should be most satisfying to him — his assurance that he will live in the works he leaves behind — occasions his most passionate exclamation:

> Thou diest while I survive?
> Say rather that my fate is deadlier still,
> In this, that every day my sense of joy
> Grows more acute, my soul (intensified
> By power and insight) more enlarged, more keen;
> While every day my hairs fall more and more,
> My hand shakes, and the heavy years increase —
> The horror quickening still from year to year,
> The consummation coming past escape
> When I shall know most, and yet least enjoy — ...   (308-17)

In contrast to the numerous end-stopped lines with which Cleon had described his rational-mechanistic view of progress (89-98), the despair he experiences before the relentless movement of time is enacted in the climactic flow of a long periodic sentence. The struggle within Cleon has reached its most critical stage, that consummation of horror toward which the warring elements in his being had been steadily advancing. Never has time been more oppressive for Cleon and never has it been so apparent that he requires more than what his intellect can provide. It would seem, at this crucial stage, that he is on the verge of a resolution of his conflict. Certainly, he has already taken the first step. Not only has he recognized his deep need but he has denounced the intellect as inadequate to satisfy that need.

The final section immediately dispels any expectation of a change in Cleon. As in the opening of the poem, it is the rational, composed Greek philosopher who speaks, revealing the full extent of his immovable pride. His determination to impose order where everything has just been shown in total disorder causes him to contradict himself flatly:

> Thou canst not think a mere barbarian Jew
> As Paulus proves to be, one circumcized,
> Hath access to a secret shut from us?
> Thou wrongest our philosophy, O king,
> In stooping to inquire of such an one ...
>   ... certain slaves
> Who touched on this same isle, preached him and Christ;
> And (as I gathered from a bystander)
> Their doctrine could be held by no sane man.   (343-47, 350-53)

It is not surprising that Cleon should reject Christianity. After all, his earlier wish that Zeus might descend to earth was shortly dismissed as pure dream. But the reason he gives for rejecting the Christian doctrine is totally inconsistent with what he has revealed in the main body of his letter. Paulus is to be ignored because he is a "mere barbarian Jew" and therefore could not possibly hold a secret inaccessible to Greek philosophy. Yet Cleon has just finished denouncing that philosophy, dramatizing its failure within himself and endorsing the natural, intuitive man for being much closer to life than he. The reader is left with the conclusion that there must be two Cleons or, more precisely, one Cleon divided into two distinct, opposing personalities. In the confessional moment constituting the body of the letter, Cleon had exposed his inner consciousness and delineated the schism between his rational self-concept and his actual feelings. In the formal, apparently non-characteristic sections which open and close the poem Browning has dramatized through structure the very division, or conflict, which Cleon elsewhere candidly relates.[8]

Almost all commentators on the poem are fond of pointing to the last line — "Their doctrine could be held by no sane man" — as representative of the irony which unifies the poem. Cleon articulates a deep need and then fails to recognize the possible solution that lies within himself. But Cleon has already shown that he *does* recognize the value of man's intuitive promptings, though his unyielding cultural pride prevents him from giving way to this dimension of himself. Like Browning's Duke of Ferrara, he chooses not to stoop, and his understated, parenthetical evidence ("gathered from a by-

70

stander") merely underscores a towering and unbending hubris. But Browning's philosophical Greek artist possesses wisdom and self-insight that the Duke never needs reckon with. The significant irony of the poem is not that Cleon fails to see within himself what he most desperately needs, but that he sees much more than he finally cares to admit. Because of his insight Cleon must forcibly delude himself, disorienting himself from the reality he seeks to avoid. The final line is ironic not because Cleon fails to realize the similarity between insanity and the emotions that might save him, but because it is his own sanity that is most open to question.

Browning's dissection of the spiritual struggles of Cleon and Karshish would not have been as confident had not the poet reached a firm conviction in his own religious faith. "Saul" is a crucial poem because it embodies the resolution of a personal conflict that would profoundly affect the poet's future development. Browning began the poem in 1845 but was forced to break off after nine stanzas when he could discover no adequate consolation for the suffering king. The song David offers in stanza nine to free Saul of a dark and miserable solitude is very similar to the vision of a creative evolutionary process which occurs in the final canto of *Paracelsus*. David reminds Saul of the harmonious spirit that animates and unites all living things, boasting Saul as its triumphant result. But, as in *Sordello*, Browning apparently was unsure how the poet's unique vision of the truth could be impressed upon lesser imaginations. The blind, dumb Saul could just as well represent the public which the poet in his role as "Maker-see" must somehow rescue from a dark and paralyzing ignorance.

The poet's solution to this problem may be seen in three intervening works — a revised *Paracelsus* (1849), *Christmas Eve and Easter-Day* (1850) and the *Essay on Shelley* (1852) — in which the Incarnation is introduced as visible testimony of the place of the Infinite within the finite and temporal.[2] In *Christmas Eve and Easter-Day* the poet considers at length and in quite doctrinal terms the significance of the Incarnation. The life and death of Christ are a manifestation of God's unselfish love for humanity, a continuous event that may be felt through a totally committed love but which fades when submitted to excessive ritual or rational inquiry.

Christmas Eve and Easter-Day are somewhat tedious poems, weighted down by theological statement and a concern for the Incarnation as historical dogma. But they trace the poet's discovery of a human symbol whereby his own intuitions could be made at once incarnate and public. Browning was now able to resume "Saul," confident that the poet's celebration of life could be shared through the promise of the Incarnation. Although Browning eventually attached no importance to the Incarnation as historical fact or

71

theological doctrine, it remained for him a central element in the emotional needs of men and women. Granting that the Christian scheme of salvation "may be a fiction," he maintained that "the life and death of Christ, as Christians apprehend them, supply something which their humanity requires, and that it is true for them."[10] That need as Browning presents it in poems such as "Saul" and, especially, in "Epilogue" to *Dramatis Personae*, arises from the individual's sense of helplessness and isolation in a world in which once stable values have crumbled before inexorable laws of change. The Incarnation fills this void by introducing into the temporal process a new value — one more human and accessible than the old and therefore in harmony with the individual's need to grow.

"Saul" has always been one of Browning's most highly regarded poems,[11] even though it is an uncharacteristic dramatic monologue. No auditor is indicated and the speaker and true subject of the poem is not Saul but David. Saul occasions David's rapturous song and serves as catalyst to his theological introspection and climactic revelation. It is the conclusiveness of the revelation which suggests that David is a spokesman for Browning and not an object of psychological analysis. In other words, the truth of the visionary experience communicated by the poem seems to be of far greater importance to Browning than a dramatic portrait of David.[12] The present moment in which David relates his experience is not as critical as the past moment that is the subject of his narration. It is this "difficult minute" (279), on which Saul's future depends, which provides David with the supreme insight that Browning means to convey.

David's first task is to rescue Saul from a deep, life-threatening depression that has devitalized the external world. His preliminary encounter with Saul is ominous, the king appearing as "A something more black than the blackness" (24). Nature, the desert's intense heat, reflects the paralysis of Saul's spirit and appears antagonistic as well ("those sunbeams like swords!" 35) until David's first song reveals the harmony between man and nature: "God made all the creatures and gave them our love and our fear. / To give sign, we and they are his children, one family here" (47-48). Next David sings of the various levels of communion among men, in whom "great hearts expand / And grow one in the sense of this world's life" (50-51). The vital energy that pulsates through man and nature, giving human life the potential for unremitting joy, should be inspiriting to Saul, who as king represents a culmination of the creative life-stream.

Though Saul has been rescued from death by David's song, he hangs between hope and despair, reluctant to embrace life. David sees that thus far his kinetic and sensuous song has merely filled Saul's cup with "the wine of this life" (130), which is inadequate to restore Saul's soul. He must reach Saul at a deeper, more personal level, focusing down from the communal life of the external world to the temporal anxieties of an immobilized self. Resuming his song, he selects the image of the fruit-bearing tree as the metaphor for man's spiritual development through the flesh. Like the tree, the body grows until only its fruit, the spirit, remains. So noble and rich is Saul's spirit that he need not despair over the limitations of mortal life or fear the effects of time:

> '. . . when age shall o'er come thee, thou still shalt enjoy
> 'More indeed, than at first when inconscious, the life of a boy.
> 'Crush that life, and behold its wine running! Each deed thou hast done
> 'Dies, revives, goes to work in the world . . .   (161-64)

Saul may draw inspiration from the knowledge that none of his past deeds will be lost but will germinate a living legacy.

David's metamorphic embodiment of time as an organic, continuous process contrasts strikingly with the mechanical, synthetic view of Cleon, who had also advanced beyond the "inconscious" and could look forward to the survival of his works. Cleon comes to regard this advance as a tragic mistake, for he discovers that, contrary to appearances, such achievements only intensify his despair. The life which his works enjoy is a mockery to their thinking, feeling creator, who can only imagine but never realize lasting joy for himself. On the threshhold of making an important discovery about himself, Cleon is prevented by intellectual pride from seeing further than he does. It is David who now stands on the threshold, awaiting the illumination that he feels helpless to provide. He has revealed the lasting splendor of Saul's accomplishments but has yet to reach the man himself. Through song David has redeemed the past for Saul, but not even the power of his love can afford to him the life which time seems to deny:

> I yearned — "Could I help thee, my father, inventing a bliss,
> "I would add, to that life of the past, both the future and this;
> "I would give thee new life together, as good, ages hence,
> "As this moment, — had love but the warrant, love's heart to dispense!"
> (233-36)

Failing to achieve this expanded moment through music, David abandons his song, the lyrical pattern of his experience, and directly examines the value of that experience. There is no danger that his approach will result in the intellectual pride which had abruptly halted Cleon's search. He has enough intelligence to realize its limitations in a universe manifesting a Higher Intelligence: "Have I knowledge? confounded it shrivels at Wisdom

73

laid bare. / Have I forethought? how purblind, how blank, to the Infinite
Care!" (245-46). Cleon had once idly imagined that Zeus descended to
earth and made known the worth of his children in time, though his rational
Greek mind immediately dismissed the fiction. David is able not only to
imagine but to realize the immanence of God, for his vision is not distorted
by a proud and skeptical intellect:

> "I but open my eyes, — and perfection, no more and no less,
> "In the kind I imagined, full-fronts me, and God is seen God
> "In the star, in the stone, in the flesh, in the soul and the clod."
> (248-50)

Simply by looking within and around himself, David perceives the creative,
ever-renewing power in the universe.

Suddenly David is confounded by the thought that appears to nearly all
of Browning's visionary characters: Is God's revelation through time too
slow to satisfy the human need for fulfillment in time? Does the human
capacity to love exceed that of God, who takes so much time?

> "Do I find love so full in my nature, God's ultimate gift,
> "That I doubt his own love can compete with it? (266-67)

But David has already seen God's creative power in this life and in his song,
which could not otherwise have found expression. If God could do all this,
certainly He will do what David himself would do:

> "Interpose at the difficult minute, snatch Saul the mistake,
> "Saul the failure, the ruin he seems now, — and bid him awake
> "From the dream, the probation, the prelude, to find himself set
> "Clear and safe in new light and new life, — a new harmony yet
> "To be run, and continued, and ended — who knows? — or endure!
> (279-83)

It is characteristic of Browning that the divine interposition David envisions
is not a disruption of temporal process but an initiation of it. An act of God
redeems the difficult minute, transforming it into the infinite moment. David
thus realizes that man's suffering has meaning; what man would do, God
certainly *will* do: "Would I suffer for him I love / So wouldst thou — so
wilt thou!" (300). Where the intellectual pride of a Cleon prevails, "most
progress is most failure." Only the courageous and sacrificial love of David
begets a greater result:

> " . . . O Saul, it shall be
> "A Face like my face that receives thee; a Man like to me,
> "Thou shalt love and be loved by for ever: a Hand like this Hand
> "Shall throw open the gates of new life to thee! See the Christ stand!"
> (309-12)

David's tentative vision of a new life running on endlessly in time (283) is confirmed by the Incarnation, an event converting transcendental longing to purposeful living.

Thus Browning, after working out the temporal implications of the Incarnation, was able to provide David with a consolation for the suffering king and to complete the poem that had troubled him ten years earlier. As in "Epilogue" to *Dramatis Personae* and "Karshish," it is the face of Christ that fills the void of a vast, impersonal universe and offers new life to humanity. At the difficult minute David discovers that the power of God to provide the enduring moment is inseparable from the power of human love. In the last stanza David returns home, fully awakened to a vital universe. Through the revelation arising from his love for Saul, David is able to sense the whole earth respond to "the new law" (331), to the incarnate Spirit that animates all living things.

II

The Moment Lived: Monologues on Love

William Phelps called Browning the "poet of love," for "this passion is the motive power of his verse, as he believed it to be the motive power of the universe."[13] The close identification of human love with the evolving spiritual power in the universe made it imperative to Browning that all be risked for love. Failure to do so would isolate the individual from the creative life-stream and result in atrophy of the soul. The Duke and the lady of "The Statue and the Bust" fail to act upon a mutual passion and consequently damn their souls. The statue and the bust prove not to be commemorative testimonies to their love, as they had hoped, but are instead mocking alter egos virtually indistinguishable from the originals. The lady sees she "did no more while her heart was warm / Than does that image" (179-80) and, after comparing herself with her bust, concludes "A lady of clay is as good" (186). The Duke realizes that he is a soulless shell like his statue, which will provoke him to "laugh in his tomb / At idleness which aspires to strive" (212-13). Both are guilty of betraying their best selves, an infidelity of more serious consequence than the adulterous union averted through passivity.

In "Dîs aliter Visum" Browning again examines the consequences to souls which fail to love at the critical moment. The woman speaker addresses an older artist whose pride had allowed the moment ten years ago to slip by. Characteristically, Browning's point is not so much that a single past mistake condemns an individual to present misery. It is more apt to be the fear of making a mistake that sentences the self to a disembodied, atemporal void. Had the artist heeded the promptings of his soul and acted upon his love, he might have made "time break" (117) "into eternity" (119), initiating a "wise beginning, here and now" which "heaven must finish, there and then" (123). His failure to act has brought despair not only to their two souls but to those of the mates they eventually selected.

Critics have usually treated "The Last Ride Together" as a representative statement of Browning's philosophy of love. Edward Berdoe said that the speaker uses his ideal to sublimate and expand his soul "til it almost becomes divine": "The force of the hour, the value of the quintessential moment as factors in the development of the soul, have never been set forth, even by Browning, with such startling power."[14] William DeVane, in the *Handbook*, called the speaker "one of Browning's incredibly noble rejected lovers."[15] More recently, Dallas Kenmare has indicated that the speaker grows to a great stature through loving,[16] and Norton Crowell has stated that he is "sustained by a durable philosophy uncommon in adversity."[17] Admittedly the speaker echoes familiar Browning themes — the perpetual striving after an unattainable goal and the experiencing of an "instant made eternity." But to take these ideas out of context, thereby ignoring the dramatic voice of the poet, is to invite a serious misreading of the poem.[18]

The impression that Browning is always concerned with imparting a particular "message" has frequently diverted readers' attention from characterization. In no other poem does Browning's practice more fully bear out a statement of Chesterton's: "Everything that was profound, everything, indeed, that was tolerable in the aesthetes of 1880, and the decadent of 1890, has its ultimate source in Browning's great conception that everyone's point of view is interesting, even if it be a jaundiced or a bloodshot point of view."[19] In "The Last Ride Together" the speaker could just as well be a *fin de siècle* decadent for his nihilistic rejection of past and future and total commitment to his immediate sensory experience. It is not the development of the speaker's soul or a sublime expression of romantic love that provides the chief interest of the poem but the speaker's desperate attempt to rationalize his failure. The reader becomes involved in the ride itself, as the speaker makes his frantic run against time (it is, after all, his *last* ride) and then climactically attempts to stop time.

In the opening stanza the speaker, a rejected lover, indicates that he accepts his "fate" and bids his former mistress take back the hope she had once given him. Good sport that he is, he claims only a memory of her and permission for one more ride. But in the next stanza this gentlemanly gesture gives place to a recklessly selfish, Epicurean hope. The last ride represents no affectionate leave-taking for him but reflects his mindless dependence on the pleasures of the instant: "Who knows but the world may end to-night?" (22). The subsequent movement of the poem presents merely an intensification of this attitude. There is no genuine development in the speaker's thoughts nor is there the acquisition of new or deeper understanding at the end. The speaker's mad attempt to stop time, thus fixing an ecstatic moment, is the whole and sufficiently compelling experience conveyed by the poem.

The speaker's riding should not be mistaken for the striving which he characterizes as so much wasted effort. It is clearly a heaven on earth that he envisions, for the image of the descending cloud in stanza three suggests that he has no idea of the elevation love can bring to the soul which aspires toward it. Aspiring is out of the question, for his riding fixes him in one place. It arises from no point in the past and aims toward no goal in the future.

As the ride gets underway in stanza four, the speaker's decision to ignore the past enables him to view his soul as "a long-cramped scroll" suddenly unwinding and "fluttering in the wind" (36). For the poet who once said his only concern was to portray incidents in the development of a soul, the unwound scroll could only be the image of a life-story abruptly voided. The difficult process by which the individual evolves a true self is aborted once the experience of the past — however painful — is denied. "Fluttering" suggests the meaningless but distracting activity by which the speaker would eliminate any regrets for a wasted life. Like the lovers of "The Statue and the Bust" and "Youth and Art" he has evaded the risk that love demands. But he rationalizes that if he has not won the lady, neither has he completely lost her, as evidenced by their riding together.

In stanzas five through eight he gives further rationale for preferring riding to striving. The choice between "This present" and "the hopeful past" (54) is an easy one for the speaker, who endorses his present activity: "I hoped she would love me; here we ride" (55). The disparity between man's longings and his physical limitations — "What act proved all its thought had been? / What will but felt the fleshly screen?" (58-59) — also testifies that "riding is better" (66). No one should be more aware of this dichotomy than the artist himself, whose limitless imagination renders him especially vulnerable to temporal restrictions. The speaker mocks the poet with the paradox Cleon had found so hard to accept:

> . . . you expressed
> You hold things beautiful the best,
> And pace them in rhyme so, side by side.

>'T is something, nay 't is much: but then,
>Have you yourself what's best for men?
>Are you — poor, sick, old ere your time —
>Nearer one whit your own sublime
>Than we who never have turned a rhyme? (69-76)

The speaker's cynical remarks concerning the dedicated poet, sculptor, and musician may be a clue to his own character, for he adds: "I gave my youth; but we ride, in fine" (88). The sudden juxtaposition of past and present in this line affords a glimpse of the whole man, whose sense of frustration and failure appears to stem from more than unrequited love. Having failed to strive, the speaker now grasps at riding as the next best thing.

In stanza nine the speaker abruptly treats the ride as a quest toward some higher life, but this apparent inconsistency in his argument is only a strategic turn anticipating his conclusive renunciation of the quest notion in stanza ten. In this final stanza he betrays his underlying attitude, admitting to the vain wish that has been at the back of his mind:

>What if heaven be that, fair and strong
>At life's best, with our eyes upturned
>Whither life's flower is first discerned,
>We, fixed so, ever should so abide? (101-04)

By freezing himself and his beloved in time, the speaker's self-betrayal is as complete as the spatial fixation of self practiced by the Duke in "The Statue and the Bust." The infinite moment proves equally elusive to both characters, whose love is jaded by a denial of the soul's potential for growth. Browning's infinite moments occur when the crucial moment takes on duration, when the whole of the past is transmuted into the onward movement of the present where it shares in the creation of the future. The speaker's last wish for a heaven of perpetual riding, for "the instant made eternity," is futile since past and future are excluded. Yet the ending of the poem does not force an immediate judgment against him. Still caught up in the experience of the ride, the reader is unlikely to question its deeper justification. The poet has welded emotional and intellectual matter so convincingly that he manages to submerge any concerns over the disproportion between the emotional statement and the troublesome intellectual idea. While the skillful use of imagery, rhythm, and repetition sustains the movement of the ride, the speaker's carefully controlled argument provides all the justification the reader needs to yield to its impetuous course. In fact, the persistent tendency of readers to applaud "The Last Ride Together" as something it is not — a profound love poem or a noteworthy expression of the philosophy of the imperfect — is an ironic, if not perverse, testimony to the success of that argument.

During the ride the speaker cautiously avoids any direct endorsement or defense of riding. Instead he points out unpleasant alternatives in stanzas four through ten and then lifts our spirits as, in the concluding line of each stanza, he allows us to ride by each. Everything will be all right, he seems to assure us, since "we ride, in fine." By the time he does reveal his own position through the provocative concluding question, he has us fully entranced with the joys of riding. Rather than shake our heads over his vain question we are inclined to obey its suggestiveness and to succumb to the illusion ourselves.

Love in Browning's poetry demands recognition of a dynamic, evolving time in which the present is inseparable from past and future. Through the speaker in "The Last Ride Together," however, Browning portrays a totally escapist attitude toward time. In the rejected lover's specious argument, the experience itself, and not the fruit of experience, is the end; therefore, the brevity of the ecstatic moment does not immediately appear problematic. By presenting the speaker's shallow rationalizations as a concluding open question — Isn't heaven merely the present instant eternally prolonged? — Browning is challenging the reader eventually to supply the problematic idea.

Browning's close awareness of the effects of time upon a human relationship makes him one of the most satisfying of all English poets on the subject of married love.[20] Intense passion between a man and a woman is of little value unless it can meet the test of time. At each critical moment selfish considerations must be overcome and love reenacted in order for a relationship to benefit from the evolutionary character of time. Repeatedly, however, pride and selfish interests interfere, causing time to assume a hostile, destructive character. The speaker in "The Last Ride Together" merely struggles to erase the past in order to assert a selfish, one-sided interest. As a result, he, like Porphyria's lover, becomes engaged in a futile effort to isolate and preserve one instant. In "Two in the Campagna" the speaker wishes that the life freely manifested by nature would inspire two souls to love. But intellectual abstraction prevents him from sustaining "the good minute." Like many Browning characters, the speaker is left with frustration over his inability to put the infinite within the finite:

> Only I discern —
> Infinite passion, and the pain
> Of finite hearts that yearn. (58-60)

Through a cycle of nine poems the speaker in *James Lee's Wife* attempts to understand time's devastating effects upon the love she had formerly shared with her husband. In the first five poems nature is bleak and desolate, a wintry, lifeless analogue to the speaker's own soul:

> But why must cold spread? but wherefore bring change
> To the spirit,
> God meant should mate his wife with an infinite range . . .   (III, 75-77)

In the sixth poem the speaker perceives that "the limit time assigns" may possibly be a probationary measure God offers for man's own good:

> Rejoice that man is hurled
> From change to change unceasingly,
> His soul's wings never furled!   (219-21)

Eventually she comes to realize that self-pity over her unrequited love would duplicate the selfish detachment of her husband. She will temper the infinite longings of her soul to the successive movement of time:

> "Shall earth and the cramped moment-space
> "Yield the heavenly crowning grace?
> "Now the parts and then the whole!"   (VIII, 320-22)

The speaker of "Any Wife to Any Husband" is another woman anxious to assure herself that a deeply shared love, for which she has "one little hour to thank" (48), will be able to withstand the advances of time. Her faith that time makes everything old while "soul makes all things new" (18) deserts her when she sees that her husband prefers younger faces to her fading beauty. Even her final desperate hope that his pride will keep him true disappears: "Pride? — when those eyes forestall the life behind / The death I have to go through!" (121-22). In denying the past he had already proven his failure to grow through love.

Although in all these poems time is shown to be disruptive of the passion between man and woman, for Browning the fulfillment of such passion is possible only because of time. "By the Fireside" has been called "the greatest love poem in the English language,"[21] and perhaps deservedly so. In no way does the shared experience which the poem presents seem to be qualified by the viewpoint of the male speaker and, because the poem is dramatic, neither does it seem limited by the perspective of the poet himself. At the height of the climactic "infinite moment" the speaker expresses the mystic irony — "One near one is too far" (230) — which dissolves individual perspectives and effects the fusion of two souls into "our one soul." Since the life of this one soul is the exclusive subject of the poem, "By the Fireside" is, in the truest sense, an anatomy of love itself. Browning has managed to subordinate all conflicting elements to the shared experience which constitutes his understanding of love.

The situation is parallel to that in "Dîs aliter Visum," for in both poems the speaker retraces the path to a critical moment in the past. This nostalgic turn is rare in Browning, for whom the endurance of love requires that time be experienced as ceaseless becoming, as a creative process in which the past is a dynamic element in the present. The speaker of "By the Fireside" wonders how he may even "dare pursue / The path gray heads abhor" (104-05). For most, it leads to a futile coveting of the past and an aversion to the present. In "Dîs aliter Visum" the speaker's retrospective effort uncovers the fossil, merely, of an unfulfilled love and the consequent fragmentation of the lives concerned. In "By the Fireside" the speaker and his wife may take the backward path only because it confirms the spiritual evolution of their common soul:

> My own, confirm me! If I tread
>   This path back, is it not in pride
> To think how little I dreamed it led
>   To an age so blest that, by its side,
> Youth seems the waste instead?
>
> My own, see where the years conduct!
>   At first, 'twas something our two souls
> Should mix as mists do; each is sucked
>   In each now: on, the new stream rolls ...   (201-09)

They need not fear the past for it is included in the dynamic stream of the present, which has grown out of the specific past experience toward which the speaker is constantly moving. But while the chronological movement of the poem is backward, the poet achieves a sense of advancing from the present into a future which contains something as yet unknown to both speaker and reader.

The mysterious fourth stanza gives some idea of the complexity of Browning's chronology:

> I shall be at it indeed, my friends:
>   Greek puts already on either side
> Such a branch-work forth as soon extends
>   To a vista opening far and wide,
> And I pass out where it ends.

In other words, the poet places in the future the circumstances of the past imaginary experience he proceeds to relate in the present. The stanza thus serves as an effective transition into the sense of creative flux which the speaker wishes in part to convey. In stanzas I-III he had indicated that he would be found over his "great wise book," "deep in Greek," when autumn came. Since Greek is no doubt an associative image for Browning's wife, herself a Greek scholar, the poet is able to experience time differently because of the unique quality of their relationship. Without abandoning the concrete moment of the opening stanza the speaker is enabled to extend his consciousness in both directions from this moment. "Greek puts already on either side / . . . a branch-work forth," giving the speaker free passage to either side — past or future. In this case, the end of the passage is merely the limit line which marks the speaker's crossing over from a spatial continuum — with its chronological sequence of before and after — to a world of duration — with its dynamic interpenetration of past, present, and future.

In stanza V, the speaker, joined by his companion, descends into the past: "And we slope to Italy at last / And youth, by green degrees" (24-25). The quest is organized around the "ruined chapel" that initially appears high up in the alpine gorge but soon occupies a place just opposite the bridge which lies before them. Before advancing further, the speaker turns to his wife for the first time, addressing her in the present tense but in the future situation he had projected in stanza I. He has discovered enough to interrupt his journey in the past, the subject of his future recollection, and to anticipate its outcome ("'t was something our two souls / Should mix as mists do" 127-28). The fullness of a love shared in time telescopes tense distinctions into the moment of the speaker's meditations. Yet he reveals that the meaning of this moment remains to be disclosed:

> Think, when our one soul understands
>   The great Word which makes all things new,
> When earth breaks up and heaven expands,
>   How will the change strike men and you . . .   (131-34)

Just as the speaker's present moment contains the extremes of past and future, the awaited change combines the opposites of foreclosure and disclosure, of death and renewal. Unable to gain further insight into the meaning of this disturbing, anticipated apocalyptic moment, the speaker and his companion resume their journey, crossing the bridge leading to the chapel. Having peered inside, they are about to return across the bridge when the speaker cautions, " — but wait!" (180), and announces, "Oh moment, one and infinite!" The moment takes on duration because both persons have fully responded to its challenge. The speaker knows that "Had she willed it, still had stood the screen / So slight, so sure, 'twixt my love for her" (196-97). His own sacrifice is like that of a tree asked to shed all its leaves but unable to throw off the last leaf, even though its loss is something "the year can mend" (209). His good fortune is for the leaf to "unfasten itself" (209) and find its "dwelling place" (214) in his companion's heart. Nothing is forced; nothing depends on self-conscious effort. Because at the critical moment each had vanquished even the smallest remnant of selfishness, their union attains the mystic oneness which often eludes Browning's lovers:

> If two lives join, there is oft a scar,
>   They are one and one, with a shadowy third;
> One near one is too far.   (228-30)

The speaker now feels capable of answering his earlier question concerning the effects of change upon love (134). The temporal order need pose no threat, he has just discovered, for

> all we perceive and know in it
> Tends to some moment's product thus,
>   When a soul declares itself — to wit,
> By its fruit, the thing it does!   (242-45)

If the significant moment is the fruit of human actions, there is no need to regard it nostalgically, to isolate or guard it. Petrifaction produces putrefaction. By resuming his journey and acting freely in time the speaker had afforded to the moment the duration that "forwards the general deed of man" (247). Since the moment increases rather than fades, the speaker may confidently assert, "I *am* named and known by that moment's feat" (251). The poet no longer senses apprehension over the future for the apocalyptic moment has been brought into the present. The "moment's feat" is not merely an event in the speaker's past but it is at once the speaker's loving act and the poem itself, the actual performance of the poet, whose soul even now "declares itself — to wit, / By its fruit, the thing it does!"

In the final three stanzas the poet, reversing the temporal sequence of the opening stanzas, moves through the various time depths of the poem back to the concrete present. In stanza LI he still recalls the past and the chapel, and in stanza LII he is back at the fireside, sharing a quiet moment with his wife in their advanced age. Then, in the concluding stanza, his reference to the concrete moment of the present cancels out all other moments depicted in the poem:

> And the whole is well worth thinking o'er
>   When autumn comes: which I mean to do
> One day, as I said before.   (263-65)

The irony in these lines is not simply that the poet has already done what he only *means* to do. He has, in effect, done much more. Rather than "thinking o'er" the whole and forming a reflective statement, he has, by fitting the entire poem to one momentary perception, given the reader a direct and intimate feeling of the whole.

The Moment Saved: Monologues on Art

As a celebrant of human existence, intent on showing men and women how to find meaning and fulfillment in a mutable world, Browning saw in art the means of providing the necessary vision. Art has no value as an end in itself; its function is to strip away illusions fabricated by intellect and lay bare the truth. Music is the highest art form for Browning because it is a direct embodiment of his temporal universe, but all great art aspires to afford the individual a glimpse of the same creative life-stream. Toward this end, the artist as "maker-see" must override self-protective defenses and place himself within the object his art depicts.

Browning's theory of art follows closely, then, upon his view of love, both of which are based on his understanding of time as duration, or continuous becoming. The function of art is to intimate the dynamic, purposeful whole which, through an aspiring love, may be directly experienced. To the artist love comes first; one must live duration in order to express it. In "Youth and Art" Browning contrasts the proud and vain idealism of youthful artist-Bohemians with the unselfish effort demanded by love. Because the two artists hold their careers too precious to jeopardize with an inconvenient, potentially problematic relationship, they fail to attain either personal or artistic fulfillment. Their calculating natures have subjugated their truest passions, making their fame and success an empty, dubious achievement.

In "Old Pictures in Florence" the history of painting is viewed within a progressive, evolutionary context. By isolating and crystallizing a single moment, Greek art achieved a perfection of external form at the expense of further growth. The art of the early Italian masters, however, discovered in time a value that had eluded the understanding of the Greeks:

> To-day's brief passion limits their range;
> It seethes with the morrow for us and more.
> They are perfect — how else? they shall never change:
> We are faulty — why not? we have time in store.
> The Artificer's hand is not arrested
> With us... (121-26)

The words "in store" initiate a play of meanings based on the double sense of an accumulated reserve and of a pending action. Viewing time not as completion or loss but as duration, the Italian masters reflect a creative earliness defying their historical belatedness. In protest against the petrifaction manifest in Greek art the early Italian painters decided to paint human nature just as they found it in order to uncover the dynamic reality, " 'To bring the invisible full into play!' " (151).

Browning's Fra Lippo Lippi epitomizes this new realism in art. He is determined to paint things, their "changes, surprises" (285), "just as they are" (294) in order to reveal that the world "means intensely, and means good" (314). Although his superiors, representing the fixed authority of the past, direct him to forget flesh and to paint only the souls of men, Fra Lippo sees nothing to prevent him from making "his flesh liker and his soul more like, / Both in their order" (207-208). In finding soul closely bound up with matter and equally affected by the movement of time, he ironically sees much more of spirit than does the Prior, whose dogmatic mind limits him to a strictly materialist perspective ("Man's soul, ... it's a fire, smoke ... no, it's not ... / It's vapour ... ' " 184-85). The Prior's stumbling hypostatizations of the intangible contrast with Fra Lippo's soul-revealing temporalizations of the world of sensory experience. Lippo has lived time as duration and experiences the totality of his past life as a living part of the present ("my whole soul revolves, the cup runs over" 250). Consequently, he cannot renounce his worldly experience and retreat to a dead past as his superiors demand:

> ... my lesson learned,
> The value and significance of flesh,
> I can't unlearn ten minutes afterwards.   (267-69)

The evaluative terminology that figures prominently in Lippo's monologue indicates an interpretative disagreement that goes fundamentally deeper than it first may seem. His conflict with the authorities is not so much over the meaning of what is depicted as over the meaning of meaning. In characterizing the abstract and rigidly formal art of the Prior, Lippo points up their differing understandings: " ... any sort of meaning looks intense / When all beside itself means and looks nought" (203-04). For Lippo it is the "all beside" in which meaning is to be sought. His meaning lacks the fixed didactic intensity prescribed by the Prior: " ' ... when your meaning's plain / It does not say to folk — remember matins, / Or, mind you fast next Friday!' " (317-19). Instead, Lippo's is a meaning in the making, elusive because it is bound up with the temporality of a dynamic creation (283-85). To the Prior's fully disclosed and completed meaning merely awaiting a skilled graphic designer, Fra Lippo opposes a meaning that is always yet to be found (315).

Although Lippo has absorbed much of the language of the establishment that he must answer to, the semantic referents he employs are often different. At the same time Lippo is fully aware of the approved virtues signified by objects which in his own mind are signs of a lower, even ludicrous, order. This double awareness, which produces in Lippo a deceptive use of verbal expression as well as visual representation, has led to confusion in interpreting the precise nature of the conflict he experiences. Especially problematic is the meaning of his about-face in the last section of the poem, when the mercurial monk appears to cast doubt on all he has said by suddenly admitting that he has spoken idly and in haste. He is then seen in an almost despicable light as he attempts to bribe his captors not to report him to the monastery. The bribe he offers is a painting — which he plans to contribute to the Church — of a Madonna and child, "Ringed by a bowery flowery angel-brood" (349) and with "a saint or two" (353) in the foreground for good measure. In a corner of the painting will appear Lippo himself, a blushing voluptuary apparently shamed by "this pure company" (368). A common theory concerning Lippo's behavior at this point is that the monk reverses his philosophy and violates his beliefs so that Browning can prevent the dramatic form of his character study from becoming a philosophical disquisition.[22]

Certainly a tension between sympathy and judgment, as Robert Langbaum has explained,[23] frequently characterizes our response to the speakers of Browning's dramatic monologues. Pictor Ignotus, a painter who practices the philosophy of art held by Lippo's superior, would be no more sympathetic than the Prior had not Browning counterbalanced the implied criticism of Pictor's position with a compassionate understanding of the man himself. But the poet may introduce tension and maintain dramatic interest in character without making the character appear inconsistent or at odds with himself. The conflict in Lippo need not be one "between flesh and spirit,"[24] or between equally strong attractions to "two worlds, the monastery and the street."[25] Nor, as has more recently been suggested, does Lippo necessarily seem polarized by a struggle between a "Prior-within" and an "authentic, original Beast," an antagonism between a "flesh-denying" and a "flesh-affirming" self.[26] Lippo has revealed his unmistakable preference to us and shown, moreover, that his choice precludes any problematic dichotomy of body and soul. The basic conflict is between Lippo's artistic convictions and his awareness of the formidable external authority which represses them. This is the conflict that motivates and sustains Fra Lippo's account of himself and influences his behavior at the end of the poem. Despite his determination to paint what experience had taught him — the value and significance of flesh — he may not do so without enduring the disapproval of his superiors: " '... the old grave eyes / Are peeping o'er my shoulder as I work, / The heads shake still — "It's art's decline, my son!' " (231-33). Although Lippo submits to their patronizing, fatuous judgment and paints to please them, he preserves his integrity through sarcasm ("Don't you think they're the likeliest to know / They with their Latin?" 241-42) and an attitude of bitter defiance ("I swallow my rage, / Clench my teeth, suck my lips in tight, and paint" 242-43). In the final section it is this same sarcasm and defiance that prevail as Lippo appears to debase himself in order to placate the authority that once more attempts to judge him. Lippo is a con artist like many other Browning speakers, but unlike, say, an Andrea, a Guido or even a Duke of Ferrara, the ultimate deceit he practices is not upon himself. Rather than expend his creative energies on rational defenses that permit an evasion of his actual self, he confronts the living self directly while at the same time taking the necessary measures to insure its survival. He has been a con artist so that he might be an artist, and his performance before the night watch is a representation of his life quest, an open-ended, "good" moment in which he seconds his true self.

In placing himself within his own painting, then, Fra Lippo maintains his artistic identity. Even though he submits to narrow, vulgar tastes, he manages at the same time to inject some of his own experience into his work, to stamp his image upon it. By now it is apparent that the painting Lippo has described is actually a strong parody of the narrow conception of religion which it represents. It is also clear that Lippo's self-disparagement ("I, in this presence, this pure company!" 368) is a device allowing him simultaneously to disarm his captors and to vent his resentment toward authority. But more than an act of defiance the painting serves as Lippo's self-portrait. The key is the "sweet angelic slip of a thing" (370), whom Lippo represents as saving him and whom he compares to the Prior's "niece." To the Prior the niece had been a concrete symbol of his repressed sensuality and hypocrisy, as Lippo makes clear:

> You tell too many lies and hurt yourself:
> You don't like what you only like too much,
> You do like what, if given you at your word,
> You find abundantly detestable.   (261-64)

To Fra Lippo the niece is testimony to the soul that can be found even in the prettiest face; through her he may illustrate the value and significance of flesh. Clasping the palm of her who rescues him in his painting, Lippo is finally saved through his bold adherence to and practice of his deepest artistic convictions.

Browning's handling of chronological time in "Fra Lippo Lippi" is an index to the structure of his best monologues. Fra Lippo is apprehended just

87

after midnight and by the time he has finished his speech it is dawn. The credibility of this great a lapse in objective time during a relatively concentrated speech underscores Browning's ability to expand the moment beyond the limits of the form containing it. Lippo's mention of the morning star indicates that the poet has foreshortened time, used a part to suggest the whole, and for this reason "Fra Lippo Lippi" is of special interest for the techniques Browning employs to suggest an extension of the moment.

In the opening 43 lines Lippo is caught up in the immediate situation which confronts him. By interspersing his defense with quick acknowledgements of the watchmen's responses he is able to suggest very concisely the entire exchange that has followed his apprehension. In line 44 Lippo chooses to sit and level with his captors, shifting attention from the present moment to the recent circumstances which have led up to it, an account that brings him back, in line 75, to the concrete present.

Seeing that he has thus far made no persuasive impact upon his audience, Lippo once again shifts the attention away from the present and, in line 81, retreats all the way back to his early childhood. He dwells at length upon his induction at the age of eight into the monastery, allowing this central experience to reveal the substance of the first eight years of his life — years that have had the most decisive, formative influence upon his character. The circumstances of his entrance into the monastery are dramatically portrayed as if they are occurring in the present. Instead of narrating past experiences, Lippo recreates the voices of the Prior and the other monks so that they may reveal themselves.

This present-tense effect also reveals what has happened to Lippo between the time he was eight years old and the immediate present. Following one of the Prior's criticisms, Lippo, in line 198, significantly responds in the present tense: "Now is this sense, I ask?" We see that the restrictions imposed upon him at the age of eight are the same that he confronts today. Since becoming a monk, Lippo has lived out a ceaseless conflict between the store of his childhood experience and the repressive authority of the monastery. Consequently, by focusing on this central, unchanging fact of his life and by keeping it within the perspective of the present, he may advance from his childhood to the present moment without any reference to the passing of time. Were the attempt unsuccessful, the reader would have to conclude that the speaker is eight years old! But Lippo is able to move imperceptibly up to the present because he has demonstrated the inseparability of past and present: " 'Rub all out!' Well, well, there's my life, in short, / And so the thing has gone on ever since" (221-22).

Even the present moment resists definition because the pattern it fits into is in flux. Lippo speaks of the just completed moment, in which he has been apprehended, as a moment that is "pretty sure to come" (245). He has managed to suggest his whole life without specific references to chronological time, and Browning is able to use this indefinite, protracted moment to sustain the illusion of the definite amount of time that has passed while his artist-monk has been speaking. The reader senses that he has spent a full and rewarding night of it when Lippo reminds him, in line 272, that "the morning-star's about to shine."

In "Fra Lippo Lippi" Browning contrasts the early Renaissance artist's involvement with the living and actual to the medieval preference for static abstractions. In attempting to copy a world of timeless perfection, the medieval artist created an art preoccupied with fanciful distortions and hence doomed to an early death. The anonymous painter in Browning's "Pictor Ignotus," who has attempted in each of his pictures to reproduce "eternal aisles / With the same series, Virgin, Babe and Saint," is hard pressed to defend the value of his unseen pictures as they "surely, gently die!"

The early Renaissance artist, on the other hand, saw imperfection as a challenge encouraging self-realization in the here and now. The artists of the Italian *quattrocento*, as depicted in "Old Pictures in Florence" and "Fra Lippo Lippi," substitute for the anguish of human mutability a joy of being in time. The distinguishing characteristic of this new spirit, according to Georges Poulet in his *Studies in Human Time*, was the sense of time as continuous becoming: "Thus by the time of the Renaissance the whole hierarchy of forms which in the eyes of the Middle Ages constituted the permanent structure of the world had disappeared. In a universe which now seemed entirely subject to vicissitude . . . God no longer appeared to be the transcendent cause which from without preserved his creatures and their own individual and continuing existences; God seemed rather the indwelling power . . . a transforming and vivifying force which sustained the universe but which sustained it only in its becoming."[27]

Poulet's study goes on to show, however, that the art that got its impetus from the realization of human potential in a world of continuous becoming carried with it tendencies no less self-destructive than the art of the Middle Ages. Freed to celebrate sensory beauty by virtue of the discovery of an indwelling, universal spiritual force, the individual soon came to venerate the object of beauty for its own sake. Likewise the art that had proven revolutionary in its manifestation of new life came to be an object coveted for itself. John Huizinga, in *The Waning of the Middle Ages*, notes this development and places it in a later period of the Renaissance: "In the treasures of princes and nobles, objects of art accumulated so as to form collections. No longer serving for practical use, they were admired as articles of luxury and of curiosity; thus the taste for art was born which the Renaissance was to develop consciously."[28]

This separation of art from life, which Browning regarded as fatal to both, is the theme of another group of poems set in the Renaissance, including "The Bishop Orders His Tomb," "My Last Duchess," and "Andrea del Sarto." In these monologues the art originally concerned with awakening humanity to the joy of an evolving life in time has come to be valued for the suggestions of immutable beauty which permit a sense of escape from time. The attitudes portrayed in these poems represent a new phase in human responses to time. Poulet traces back to this shift the acute sense of isolation characteristic of the modern age: "With the end of the Renaissance the feeling of spontaneous intercommunication in all individual activity within the cosmic *becoming* has also disappeared. Human thought no longer feels itself a part of things. It distinguishes itself from them in order to reflect upon them, and thus is no longer upheld by their power of enduring. . . . Separated from the duration of things, and even from that of the modes of its existence, the human consciousness finds itself reduced to existence without duration. It is always of the present moment."[29]

The dying cleric in "The Bishop Orders His Tomb" is pathetic in his isolation and almost pathological in his attempt to force duration upon a moment whose contents are wholly sensual. In the critical moment of his speech, as he vainly seeks his sons' ears, the Bishop reveals a lifelong compulsion for possessing material things and a consciousness filled with an undiminished appetite for physical sensation. The tomb that he orders his sons to provide will be a final gratification to his senses — not only overshadowing the tomb of a former competitor but permitting him to enjoy the immortality that only solid marble can provide. As the clusters of images mount up in increasingly distorted and confused relationships, the Bishop's desperation becomes evident. Instead of a marble tomb the best he can expect from his sons is perishable gritstone. The illusions that have sustained the Bishop throughout life crumble before him at the critical moment of his death. Despite his urgent efforts to take with him into eternity his private world of materialism and greed, he is not protected by psychosis. The only thought that consoles him as his world disintegrates is the memory of a dead mistress who provoked his rival's envy even if his tomb will not.

The Duke of "My Last Duchess" sees his late wife in much the same light as the Bishop views his mistress — as an object of beauty capable of conferring esteem upon her possessor. The reason for the Duke's fixation upon the Duchess is not immediately apparent, however. Unlike the Bishop, who finally clings to the only comfort left him, the Duke would have the envoy regard the Duchess as just one more prize in his abundant trophy case. Moreover, the Duke is in the prime of his life. The synthetic world created by his sensual, egotistical mind appears to be in no imminent danger of collapse, yet there is in his gratuitous performance before the envoy a hint that it suffers somewhere from a crack at the seams. His gallery of museum pieces simply cannot compete with the luster of the Duchess' vibrant universe. Her delight in nature and impartial love of humanity expose the artifice of the Duke, who would not belabor a posthumous denunciation of her — however glibly — unless he still viewed her as a threat. Even the Duchess's inscrutability forces the Duke to confront limitations — he stumbles repeatedly in trying to analyze her character — that challenge his mastery over a world which he cannot own if he cannot name.

Like the Bishop, the Duke has an underlying awareness of his delusion but he also has enough vitality to discharge any personal misgiving through a performance more for his own benefit than the envoy's.[30] Both speakers prove equally incapable of regeneration at their critical moments. The Bishop cannot free himself from his materialist perspective and hence has no more power to resist the destructive force of time than does the crumbling gritstone to which his sons commit his corpse. The Duke, at a crucial juncture between duchesses, has an opportunity to introduce a new order into his life but instead lapses back into the old. By the time he bids the envoy accompany him below, he has discharged not simply guilt but his humanity as well. The statue of Neptune taming a sea-horse, which the Duke casually singles out, is no doubt an ironic commentary on the Duke's dominance and sadism, an association of which the artful Duke may even be consciously proud. But this parallel between the statue's and the Duke's dramatic situation permits a more profound paradox that finally eludes the Duke. The most revealing point of contact between the Duke and the statue is to be found in the statue's constituent. The Duke has incarcerated himself in a world of bronze and cannot see that he is finally possessed by the objects he claims to possess.

Like the Bishop and the Duke, Andrea del Sarto has spatialized flowing time, breaking it up into fragments that exist in a material world apart from self. As a result, he, too, is imprisoned in a world of delusion, as static as the Duke's and as unstable as the Bishop's. His character is at first more sympathetic than that of the Bishop or Duke because of his self-critical awareness of what he might have become. Yet it becomes increasingly clear during the

91

moments in which Andrea confronts the wasted potential of his career that each of these moments is itself another wasted chapter in his life story. At certain points he reveals surprising self-knowledge and yet at none of these instants is he capable of overcoming the rationalizations that forbid him to act. The suspicion grows that Andrea has expended his best energies circumscribing his imagination within static structures in order to forestall the challenges of a temporal existence. Immediately apparent is his uxoriousness and passivity, and the reader is likely to feel some of the same impatience as Lucrezia at being retained in his drab chamber.

Unlike Fra Lippi Lippo, whose energies constantly demand release from spatial confinement, Andrea is repeatedly attracted to protective enclosures:

> That length of convent-wall across the way
> Holds the trees safer, huddled more inside;
> The last monk leaves the garden; days decrease,
> And autumn grows, autumn in everything. (42-45)

Whereas Lippo is irresistibly drawn to the life of the street with its "changes, surprises" (285), Andrea attempts to draw about him a hermetic world in which nothing is left to chance. "Days decrease" so that time may run out, leaving Andrea with "autumn in everything," a warrant for the inevitable sterility which he prefers to feel powerless to change. Although he can regret the past and put off Lucrezia until the morning, time has ceased to exist for him. His life is a completed fact, begun and concluded by a God he conceives of as inescapable fate:

> Love, we are in God's hand.
> How strange now, looks the life he makes us lead;
> So free we seem, so fettered fast we are!
> I feel he laid the fetter: let it lie! (49-52)

As this last line suggests, the disparity between appearance and reality to which Andrea calls attention does not provoke honest frustration. His prison is, above all, a place of maximum security for himself. He sings in as well as of his chains for they spare him painful self-assessment and absolve him of responsibility for failure.

Andrea's failure as an artist is closely related to his failure as a lover; he is clearly incapable of the effort demanded by either role. Although he expresses a preference for quietly holding hands with Lucrezia throughout the evening, he hardly presses the point ("Let us but love each other. Must you go?" 219). Thus we see that his dependence upon Lucrezia stems from a need to sustain self-protecting illusions, to evade facing the truth about himself. He requires Lucrezia as a scape-goat for failure:

> 'Rafael did this, Andrea painted that:
> The Roman's is the better when you pray,
> But still the other's Virgin was his wife — '
> Men will excuse me.   (177-80)

What Andrea fails to acknowledge is that he requires Lucrezia not just as an excuse for creative impotence but for sexual as well. He has demonstrated that he takes pleasure in debasing himself before her, for the self-pity she occasions permits him to evade both the striving demanded of the great artist and the equally demanding task of making love to her.

Andrea's ploys for sympathy almost work when he gives expression to the feeling that he is somehow responsible for his condition: "Yet the will's somewhat — somewhat, too, the power — / And thus we half-men struggle" (139-40). Paradoxically, not only Andrea's will to fail but his efforts to secure the consolations of such failure are a formidable example of the self-determining power he claims to lack. Even with his added clause — "And thus we half-men struggle" — he achieves a degree of exoneration by skillfully dispersing blame that should be his alone. Although he does acknowledge the singularity of his position in comparison to artists who strive, in whom "there burns a truer light of God" (79), he is not about to relinquish the superior merit of his works, which "are nearer heaven" (87). Andrea's heaven differs from that of the speaker of "The Last Ride Together" only in that it substitutes a solemn spatial fixity for the equestrian's frenetic temporal stasis. Since the heaven Andrea confesses he would "have" (259) is merely an enlargement of his chamber — a celestial enclosure with "four great walls" (261) — his final preference for Lucrezia, however varying the responses it may provoke, certainly contains no surprises. Andrea, through his resignation to a self-designed fate and indifference to the creative possibilities in the movement of time, has wasted an artistic gift denied even the greatest of painters. His determination to shift the responsibility for his torpidity to Lucrezia incriminates him conclusively: "Had you enjoined them on me, given me soul, / We might have risen to Rafael, I and you!" (118-19). It is clear that Lucrezia is simply a reflection, not the cause, of Andrea's inadequacy in art and love. Like his paintings she is of perfect form (" — How could you ever prick those perfect ears / Even to put the pearl there! Oh, so sweet — " 27-28) but without soul.

Roma King has said of "Andrea del Sarto" that "the time element is an important part of structure."[31] Yet his subsequent analysis of the poem demonstrates how imagery, diction, syntax, rhythm, and irony are all employed by Browning to suggest Andrea's passiveness and resignation. Although Andrea talks for only half an hour as twilight yields to grayness, time appears to move much more slowly, if at all, during his speech than during Lippo's. The past which evokes Andrea's nostalgia and the future "New Jerusalem" which produces expectation in him are static entities offering merely a brief getaway from the enclosing present in which Andrea prefers to reside. Andrea, because of his isolation from the evolving movement of time, is a regressive historical figure, a latter-day painter who illustrates the "eternal petrifaction" which Browning ascribes to Greek art just as Fra Lippo Lippi is Browning's representative for the dynamic art of the early Renaissance.

This discrepancy between Andrea's attitude and his place in history permits Browning to push the irony further. Andrea has an extra amount of awareness in comparison to Cleon, who illustrates a fault common to his historical age. The enlightened perspective afforded Andrea by history enables him to see that his art is inferior for being "placid and perfect" (99), and yet he continues to venerate perfection in the person of Lucrezia, singling out her indifference and selfishness for blame. When he surrenders first place to Leonard, Rafael and Agnolo "because there's still Lucrezia" (266), then adds, "as I choose," he is accepting only limited responsibility. He has chosen not martyrdom but complacency, and the reader's final reaction could as likely be one of horror and disgust as sympathy.

Browning's mature monologues reveal the poet coming to a realization of his creative powers through the discovery of the psychological moment and its implications for self-definition and poetic form. There remained undone a work that would use not simply the moment of the speaker as the basis for a life-study but would address the immediate present of the reader, engaging him or her directly and personally in the truth-seeking process of the poem. In *The Ring and the Book* Browning attempts to generate from the present moment of the reader the moments of an obscure, distant past so that the present moment to which the reader returns will be alive and vibrant with fresh meaning from the past.

CHAPTER IV

The Poetry of Duration:
The Ring and the Book

The Ring and the Book is so vast and so essentially gothic a structure, spreading and soaring and branching at such a rate, covering such ground, putting forth such pinnacles and towers and brave excrescenses, planting its transepts and chapels and porticos, its clustered hugeness or inordinate muchness, that with any first approach we but walk vaguely and slowly, rather bewilderedly, round and round it, wondering at what point we had best attempt such entrance as will save our steps and light our uncertainty . . .

— HENRY JAMES[1]

The praise that has long been accorded *The Ring and the Book* has often had a paradoxically damning effect. In stressing the complexity and uniqueness of Browning's supreme poetic accomplishment, critics have brought the poem recognition but apparently no large number of serious readers. In a book-length study of the *Ring* Richard Altick and James Loucks suggest that the poem has been "inadequately served by criticism," especially criticism stressing a modern point of view.[2] More recently, essays by John Killham and Ian Jack have challenged the poem's claims to modernity as well as to an important place in Browning's poetic career.[3] But both critics are preoccupied with what might be regarded as Browning's moral didacticism at the expense of what the poem actually accomplishes. As Altick and Loucks maintain, " . . . the claims of *The Ring and the Book* to a high place in English poetry cannot be fairly examined until we determine what Browning actually proposed to do, and what he did: what the poem, in short, is really like ."[4]

It has been a central concern of this study to show that meaning and structure in Browning's poetry follow closely upon the poet's understanding of time as duration. *The Ring and the Book*, Browning's most comprehensive statement on human-divine relations and the problem of evil, testifies to the pervasive influence of the temporal upon the artistic process in Browning — from shaping vision to final form. In order to suggest the specific ways in which this preoccupation informs and illuminates the poem, the following discussion will begin with overall structure and then move to an

95

examination of significant characters, before concluding with a consideration of the poet's treatment of historical fact. The present chapter, while
providing no exhaustive analysis of Browning's challenging chiaroscuro, does
offer, in James's words, an "entrance as will save our steps and light our
uncertainty."

Henry James' elaborate metaphor for the "inordinate muchness" of *The
Ring and the Book* demonstrates how much easier it is to acknowledge than
examine so complex a temporal ordering. Altick and Loucks, whose *Browning's Roman Murder Story* is one of the most thorough studies of several
levels of the poem's structure, suggest that an ideal reading of the poem
"would require the suspension of time or the adoption of an extra dimension."[5] Even so, much of the poem's power, and meaning as well, depends
on the reader's participation in its total movement — a movement demanding the perception of several interrelated time processes. While each of the
monologues is in itself a unique drama of a life-in-process, each has a close,
complementary relationship with all the other monologues as well as a vital
supporting role in relation to the poem's great theme — the search within a
finite, unjust world for some evidence of an infinite, just and loving power.
Thus, the form of the poem, symbolized by the truth-seeking process of the
trial, is felt through the special, dynamic structuring of discrete but inseparable smaller units. Despite early "giveaways" by the poet and overt philoso-
phizing by the Pope the reader is allowed to see the great moral and philosophical issues of the poem evolve directly from the experiences of the
speaker, whose efforts at self-understanding extend even into the distant
past and future. Within any given moment of the poem, the reader senses
the weight of many other moments — relating not merely to the experiences
of the speaker and the other characters but to the historical-moral drama
which, as the Pope makes clear, is the trial's significant outcome, changing
the course of centuries and affecting future generations.

The language of the poem is itself an intricate, evolving process which
serves to clarify relationships and suggest broad thematic values. Altick and
Loucks find that the repeated metaphors are "both dynamic and accretive:
dynamic in that they pass through a long sequence of forms, never twice
exactly the same (a continuing emblem, therefore, of the poem's theme of
universal flux), and accretive in that with every appearance new meaning is
added to the original metaphor, each fresh occurrence involving reminis-
cence of previous forms, applications, and contexts. The same process occurs
with the referents. . . . Each element in a given metaphor contains within

96

itself the history of all its previous uses.[6] The process Altick and Loucks describe, virtually indistinguishable from Bergsonian duration, is perhaps the most apt summation of the poem's movement and import.[7] The temporal, incomplete nature of meaning and the inclusion of the past within the evolving, onward movement of the present are essential to the experience of self which it is the poet's task through language to represent. In *The Ring and the Book* Browning embodies his most characteristic convictions in a structure designed to insure the reader's participation not simply in the artist's creative act but in a process moving toward self-knowledge.

Browning's method of getting his story under way reflects his concern that the past will have a present-tense immediacy for the reader. It is not sufficient that the poet simply begin his narrative in the past, subjecting it to his imagination and enlivening it to permit the reader a willing suspension of disbelief. Rather than recreate the past, he would induce the reader to discover it as a living fact of present consciousness. The present moment of the opening lines, vividly evoked by the poet's direct address to the reader, thus becomes the key moment from which all other moments of the poem are progressively generated.

With the introductory question — "Do you see this Ring?" — the poet, by holding up his poem and forcing the reader to acknowledge its existence, shares with the reader the same moment of consciousness. Having established this affinity, the poet may take the reader into his confidence and reveal how the poem came into being, a device which simultaneously enables the poem to *come* into being. Next he invites the reader to examine the Old Yellow Book so that its physical existence can be confirmed before its contents are even considered. The detailed circumstances of obtaining the book, the motivation for selecting it among all the colorful objects of the flea market, the elation over acquiring it — all the events of this vividly evoked "memorable day" (91) take precedence over any of the events detailed within the book itself. The poet even includes a full description of the title page but does not as yet permit the reader to advance beyond it. The intensity of the poet's excitement, besides whetting the reader's appetite, has the effect of emphasizing the psychological impact of the book, shifting the focus from historical events to human consciousness, which the poet will soon establish as his true subject.

When the book is finally opened, the poet introduces the legal proceedings which account for its format. The written reports of the attorneys, the reader is made to understand, are the same documents which the court was expected to read and evaluate before pronouncing its sentence. Thus, the reader enjoys much the same perspective as the seventeenth-century court, for the "printed voice" of the attorneys "lives now as then" (167). But their testimonies, full of dry, pretentious rhetoric and professional vanity, bring the reader no closer to the central experience than the attorneys themselves were able to get. The poet insists on the written nature of his source material, not underestimating its value but also highly skeptical that the various meanings signified by the printed record can ever disclose the truth. In reporting the legal proceedings of the Yellow Book, the "untempered gold" (365), Browning realizes that he cannot hope to affect his readers' consciousness toward the facts, which in this form prove to be neither self-sufficient nor self-sustaining. He must first fuse his "live soul and that inert stuff" (469) so that past history might become a living part of present consciousness.

In preparing to come at the story a second time Browning turns from the Yellow Book to another concrete symbol of the past — the physical setting mentioned in the book. As he rediscovers in the present certain enduring landmarks and surrenders himself to each, the centuries separating him from the facts of the book suddenly dissolve:

> The life in me abolished the death of things,
> Deep calling unto deep: as then and there
> Acted itself over again once more
> The tragic piece.   (I. 520-23)

Aware of the inadequacy of a text that purports to represent stable meaning, Browning enlists the poet's imaginative alloy not to fix, and further falsify, meaning but to bring it fully into play. Moving away from the Yellow Book, the poet tells the story again (523-678), this time in a melodramatic, epic manner — St. George vs. the Prince o' the Power of the Air — so that value judgments and universal significance may be applied to the events reported in the book.

Having first briefly reviewed the facts of the tale and having then broadly indicated their human values, Browning has yet to effect the fusion which will animate the facts, transform the past into "live truth" (697). This resuscitation, he makes clear, is not simply the work of the artist but depends on the reader's participation with him in a process vital to the spiritual renewal and self-realization of both. The expressive function of the poet and the mimetic structure of the poem interest Browning far less than the reconstitutive activity of the reader, who ultimately holds the key to meaning. While the artist "repeats God's process" (717)

> No less, man, bounded, yearning to be free,
> May so project his surplusage of soul

In search of body, so add self to self
By owning what lay ownerless before, —
So find, so fill full, so appropriate forms —
That, although nothing which had never life
Shall get life from him, be, not having been,
Yet, something dead may get to live again ... (722-29)

The reader has been given to understand, then, that the past has a personal, experiential relationship with his present consciousness; moreover, he has been shown both the necessity and method of restoring it. Like the artist, the reader resists confinement in an isolated instant and mimics the creative process. It is his responsibility to *make* the meaning of the poem, first through an act of imaginative projection and then by adding, owning, finding, and appropriating the forms set forth by the poet. Thus Browning presents a third summary of events (780-823) in the form of a swift and compact factual narrative. The stage has been cleared, and into the theater of the reader's mind the poet has introduced the past, ready to "Act itself o'er anew" (825).

But first Browning must relate the plan of his poem, which does not follow the sequence of events he has already outlined. Since the subject of the poem is not simply the past dramatized, but the past as it is reflected upon in human consciousness — in the minds of the characters of the poem as well as the poet and reader — Browning now reveals the pattern of mind, his poetic structure, for ordering the living facts into a form accessible to the reader. Thus, the historical events of the poem are rehearsed a fourth time, as the poet introduces his cast of *dramatis personae* and order of speakers before giving place to the play itself. Having transferred the past into present consciousness, to act and be acted upon, the poet may finally leave the facts alone; he can now remove the alloy of fancy and trust in the self-sustaining power of the newly transformed facts. It is only fitting, then, that Browning conclude his introductory book with a purely musical passage dedicated to "lyric Love." First, the facts had been looked at as legal history, second as archetypal moral epic, third as narrative action, fourth as psychological drama, and finally, with the unveiling of the poet's ordering of fact, as song.

It is often assumed that Browning's decision to relate the plot indirectly through the reflective consciousness of his speakers deprives the poem of dramatic conflict.[8] Since Half-Rome speaks a day after the murder and each succeeding monologist speaks at a moment increasingly remote from the event, it may at first appear that time serves to lead the reader away from

99

the central crisis of the plot. Looked at another way, however, the ideation of the past and the arrangement of monologues actually contribute to dramatic tension. The critical moment at which each character speaks gains in immediacy when the monologist brings to it an awareness of a past which is also known to the reader. Browning's audience must sense a keen participation in the events of the poem if it measures, as it is challenged to do, the responses of the speaker against its own. Moreover, even though narrative and plot — the author's usual device for building suspense — have been given away, Browning has not overlooked chronology as a dramatic factor in his total structure. Just as each of the major characters, speaking at a critical moment, finds his or her truth-seeking efforts limited by time, the truth-seeking process of the entire poem is also placed under a time restriction — the execution — which silences not only Guido but all of the dramatic voices of the poem. The weight of the past thus comes increasingly to bear upon an ever narrowing present. Time itself provides the conflict which sustains the movement of the poem right up to Guido's desperate plea for help. Since Browning's focus is on neither Guido's murderous action nor the question of his guilt but rather on the character himself — the evaluation of Guido's soul, or self — this moment is the climax of the entire poem. Judgment has already been passed by the court and the Pope; now it is the reader's turn.

In the deliberately anticlimactic concluding book the poet reminds the reader that the experience of Pompilia and Caponsacchi cannot be divorced from the present. Some later evidence — the letters of Archangeli and Botini — reveals that Pompilia's public vindication was a fortunate happenstance, for her legal defense was based on lies. The sermon of Fra Celestino, contained in Bottini's letter, lays the groundwork for the poet's statement of one of the poem's major lessons — "that our human speech is nought" (XII. 838). Since a countless number of heaven's saints are lost and forgotten for every Pompilia that is rescued, we can ill afford to rest content in the knowledge that justice had been done in Pompilia's case. Celestino practically exhibits a modern deconstructionist's skepticism over the claims of speech to a more stable, present, and reliable meaning than written language. As Browning's poem has demonstrated, meaning differs from moment to moment as it defers to a truth never wholly revealed. The poet's audience has the responsibility, therefore, of never allowing its vigilance to be arrested by human speech masquerading as truth; through the dynamic language of the poem, the reader has been exercised in perceiving truth so that he or she may act to further it in the present.

Of all the characters in the poem, none tests the reader's ability to penetrate disguise more than Guido. In comparing Guido's two monologues, critics tend to leave the impression that there are two distinct characters.[9] Guido in Book V is putting on an act, we are told, for the benefit of the court but once he is beyond help, in Book XI, the sheepskin is suddenly thrown off and the wolf emerges. The transformation, however, is neither this obvious nor dramatic. A close examination of Guido's preoccupation with time in both monologues reveals a steady progression of thought and feeling within a consistently drawn character, a desperate and canny impersonator who merely exchanges one disguise for another. At the same time, he is a pathetic actor who, more than any other Browning self-deceiver, has difficulty believing in the roles he plays largely for his own benefit. The time problem which torments him in his first speech becomes his paramount concern when he speaks a second time, following the Pope's judgment, for now he is aware of the ever decreasing, certain number of moments separating him from death. The more critical the problem becomes, the more Guido is forced to adopt positions to combat it, until it finally escapes his control altogether.

Time in Guido's first speech is an abstraction, a rhetorical device removed from the moment of actual experience. Rather than the immediate moment, Guido focuses on society's debt to the elderly. Still smarting from the pain inflicted by the rack, he uses his suffering as a reminder to the judges of his age: "Sirs, / Much could not happen, I was quick to faint, / Being past my prime of life, and out of health" (V, 17-19). Such thinly disguised self-pity, which Guido claims as a minimal legacy for one deprived of youth and subject to the discomforts of advancing age, becomes the dominant tone in his defense. Having waited thirty years for preferment in Rome, he one day felt "The tick of time inside" (343) and realized he was "Hard upon, if not over, the middle of life" (346). Time, he argues, has played him for a fool, robbing him of his productive years and reducing him to failure.

Not surprisingly, it is the past which weighs most heavily in his argument before the court. His present predicament, he insists, is the direct result of the past, over which he had no control:

> Will my lords, in the plenitude of their light,
> Weigh well that all this trouble has come on me
> Through my persistent treading in the paths
> Where I was trained to go, — wearing that yoke
> My shoulder was predestined to receive,
> Born to the hereditary stoop and crease? (122-27)

Guido thus denies his freedom of will and blames heredity for his present plight, hoping this strategic use of the past will secure his freedom. Rhetorically, his question aims to arouse sympathy not only by inducing guilt but through flattery that identifies the enlightened lords with the forces of destiny. Change in the natural order has deprived him of youth, he complains, but certainly the lessons taught him by custom can not be altered, for if the court did not reward honour of birth, the entire social structure would topple.

Even more important to Guido than his noble ancestry is the law, which requires the total submission of the wife to the husband's will. For Guido, law is a fixed and dependable authority, representing "Nature, — which is God" (1171), an equation anticipating Guido's wolfish world in Book XI and exposing the materialistic basis for his actions. In a world limited to externals, rationalism prevails over intuitionism, and law becomes license for mean and selfish impulses. The Pope sees the rational basis for Guido's behavior, characterizing it as always subordinating "Revenge, the manlier sin, to interest / The meaner" (X. 600-01). It is not injured pride that motivates Guido to act but a calculating opportunism rationalized on the grounds of Darwinian necessity.

The flaw in Guido's scheme is that the fittest survivors are those who successfully challenge rather than worship nature's authority. Consequently, his natural law proves a mixed blessing, undercutting the very privileges it sanctions. When he relates that on Christmas eve he arrived in Rome, ready to "Declare to the world the one law" (1578), his law not only provides a license for self-seeking conduct but serves to heighten his frustration over time. His resentment of Pompilia's youth and his sensitivity over being past his own prime overwhelm him as everywhere he is taunted by "The Feast o' the Babe." Although he puts away his dagger and spends nine days in prayer, the problematic nature of his God-Nature identification only becomes more apparent. Having reduced God to natural law, Guido finds in the face of the Christ child simply a reflection of himself:

> The Babe's face, premature with peak and pine,
> Sank into wrinkled ruinous old age,
> Suffering and death, then mist-like disappeared ...   (1603-05)

Just as with Pompilia, whose youth eventually disgusts him, Guido associates the image of youth with its opposite. Unable to understand the flaw in his own perception which causes the Babe's face to age, Guido directs his resentment toward the offensive image itself. Thus he is confirmed in his intention of murdering Pompilia. Her death allows him to entertain the notion that he has defeated time, turned it completely backwards. The sacrifice of her youthful life has perversely restored his own:

> I am myself and whole now: I prove cured
> By the eyes that see, the ears that hear again,
> The limbs that have relearned their youthful play ...   (1707-09)

Guido realizes, however, that he cannot actually turn back the clock without the court's help. In closing his defense he reiterates his plea that his judges follow past example and vindicate him, restoring "Customs that recognize the standard worth" (41). Thus he depends on the fixity of the past to clear him of responsibility for the present. Anxious that the past not be upstaged by the present, he implores the court, "Take my whole life, not this last act alone, / Look on it by the light reflected thence!" (1786-87). But the Pope's response makes it clear that Guido's attempted evasion will not succeed:

> ... I stand already in God's face
> And hear "Since by its fruit a tree is judged,
> Show me thy fruit, the latest act of thine!
> For in the last is summed the first and all, —
> What thy life last put heart and soul into,
> There shall I taste thy product." I must plead
> This condemnation of a man to-day.   (X. 340-46)

The dynamic relationship of past and present, essential to the creative process which permits the evolution of an authentic self, is unrecognized by Guido, whose life consequently condemns itself. The Pope's judgment simply confirms the moral stagnation that has already claimed Guido as its victim.

Following the Pope's judgment, Guido in Book XI is tortured by the question, "Why do things change?" (265). The frustration he expressed earlier over the passing of his youth is now compounded with the realization that traditional standards of law and religion have also yielded to time. The Pope's decree, in ignoring the precedents Guido had counted on, has put the past out of reach and restricted the present to a tenuous twelve hours. Despite Guido's desperate plea "to live the natural minute more" (X. 178), the Pope has supported the demand that "his poor sole remaining piece of time / Be plucked from out his clutch" (X. 189-90).

The increased desperation Guido experiences in his second monologue is reflected in the temporal ordering of the speech. While addressing the judges in Book V, with the prospect of acquittal in mind, he organized the events preceding the murder chronologically so that he might emphasize all the past circumstances which should promote his release. When he speaks a second time, however, chronology is disrupted by the shock, resentment and panic which beset him as he tries to account for his present dilemma before time runs out.[10] Six times he refers to the mere twelve hours allotted him and is ever mindful that, while he is talking, sunset and the dreaded mannaia, the engine of his execution, draw nearer. The disorderly movement of Guido's second account not only underscores the greater mental stress he is under but also helps the poet to foreshorten the time of the speech. Although it is totally implausible that Guido would require twelve hours to deliver his monologue, the frequent digressions into the past, each followed by an abrupt awakening and return to the present, make dramatically acceptable the sense that much precious time has slipped away while he was digressing.

The primary thematic link with the first speech is Guido's repeated juxtaposition of past with present, followed by a denunciation of the latter on the basis of a discrepancy which the comparison reveals. It seems to Guido that if the present is suddenly going to take exception to the old, established patterns, he should at least be informed "that the law o' the game is changed" (XI. 116). As the metaphor suggests, the only change Guido can comprehend is in tactics rather than in fundamental values or beliefs.

Since repentance would not affect the death sentence, Guido will have none of it. In this respect he resembles the morally significant characters of the poem. The Pope is not anxious for Guido's confession, and the dying Pompilia, it will be seen, disproves Guido's scoffing conjecture that she forgives him. Guido's constant refusal to repent serves, then, to establish an attitude not so much against Guido as against the society represented by the Abate and the Cardinal, who encourage his repentence. As Guido tells his auditors, repentance has merely become a tool serving the narrow interests of a selfish few in an age which has supplanted God's law with man's. If ever faith was "suffered to live its little tick of time, / 'Tis dead of age, now, ludicrously dead; / Honour its ashes" (XI. 560-62).

The Pope's disregard for forgiveness in his judgment upon Guido places him in partial agreement with Guido. Both see repentance as part of the "machinery" of the age, but the Pope's decisive act, a clear break with custom, signifies a repudiation of the static order Guido imagines is unalterably established. Despite the Pope's Arnoldian distaste for the machinery of his age, he refuses to retreat in time. Instead the present corrupt system helps lay the groundwork for the next age, to be evolved from the "dread machinery" (X. 1375) of the old. In fact, the Pope's very employment of such a machine in the execution of Guido provides the cornerstone.

Thus, while Guido and the Pope see with equal penetration into the hypocrisy and corruption of their age, their differing responses can be attributed to their respective attitudes toward time. Guido, who identifies God with Nature, must regard all material change as ultimate and final. Time is synonymous with natural law, which converts individual life into death, as attested by the stockpile of ashes from the past. Contrasting sharply with Guido's aversion toward change and his consequent fatalism is the Pope's undaunted faith in change as the means by which the truth will at last be evolved. The Pope repudiates, first of all, Guido's God-Nature identification: "Mind is not matter nor from matter, but / Above, — leave matter then, proceed with mind!" (X. 1353-54). Not until reality is disencumbered of an exclusive materialistic bias is it possible to move to an intelligence capable of apprehending a world of spirit. Like David, in Browning's "Saul," the Pope trusts human intelligence to mirror a supreme creative intelligence. The evidence for this spiritual reality is perplexing to human minds because of its multiplicity and mutability, yet the Pope affirms the unity behind such diversity, a diversity which is really

> Only truth reverberate, changed, made pass
> A spectrum into mind . . .
> . . . — the same truth
> In a new form, but changed in either case.   (1391-92, 1397-98)

Guido, who knows well the mind of the man to whom he is so completely known, guesses at and almost parallels the Pope's words on the subject of change:

> Respite me, save a soul, then, curse the world!
> "No," venerable sire, I hear you smirk,
> "No: for Christ's gospel changes names, not things,
> Renews the obsolete, does nothing more!   (XI. 360-63)

But this approximation is, of course, a distortion of the Pope's actual statement. So convinced is Guido of a static and unregenerate human nature that any reference to non-material change strikes him as a euphemistic hoax. Thus, he translates the Pope's emphasis on change into simply another attempt to reclaim the past, to renew the obsolete through some form of "retinkered law" (364). Guido remains satisfied that the only necessary faith is "faith in the present life" (725), a present which is no more than a prolongation of the past. Most human beings, especially the clergy, support in one form or another his "creed's one article":

> "Get pleasure, 'scape pain, — give your preference
> To the immediate good, for time is brief,
> And death ends good and ill and everything!"   (768-70)

105

The Pope, however, clearly rejects such an attitude toward time as childish, offering in its place a stern corrective:

> We are not babes, but know the minute's worth,
> And feel that life is large and the world small,
> So, wait till life have passed from out the world.   (X. 1427-29)

Those who feel as the Pope find the moment valuable because of its duration rather than its brevity. Not even death can affect it, for its boundaries exceed the natural limits assigned this world. This "foremost fact" (1435) is grasped by those who substitute a far-sighted, courageous faith for narrow creeds of utilitarianism. The moment then becomes "the divine instance of self-sacrifice / That never ends and aye begins for man" (1657-58). Thus, the dynamic, creative character of time is revealed only to those who make the active response demanded by faith. Guido, who in the Pope's judgment "sleeps sound because the clock is vigilant" (457), becomes a victim of the clock through his complacency. Anticipating his defense before God, he offers an excuse which is ironically a self-indictment: "I am one huge and sheer mistake, — whose fault? / Not mine at least, who did not make myself?" (XI. 939-40).[11]

In the few moments remaining, Guido voices his perplexity over the change that engulfs him. If the mutable natural order decrees his eventual death, then how dare the stagnant religious-moral order seek to deprive him of life prematurely. If Pompilia's youth had wronged him, painfully reminding him of the limitations of old age —

> . . . myself am old,
> O' the wane at least, in all things: what do you say
> To her who frankly thus confirms my doubt?   (998-1000) —

then his crime merely reflected the swine-like greed and lust of the Church. As seen by Guido, the Church practices deceitfully the same primitive religion he embraces. It must dispose of him because his indiscreet actions threaten to expose the entrenched, old paganism which crudely masquerades as Christianity. The idea that the Church desires of him final repentance, or change of heart, seems, therefore, absurd. He remains adamant in his position, desiring only to "glut the wolf nature" (2060), to practice his pagan religion without further deceit. For Pompilia he would substitute a bride of his own faith, preferably a Lucrezia, a switch echoing his earlier insistence on a gospel that "changes names, not things."

Returning to his approaching execution, Guido avers that he draws strength from his wolf-nature, that he is "careless, gay even" toward death (2331), since sooner or later the final minute comes even to the most cautious of men, pricking "At lazy heart" and "torpid brain" (2364). Perhaps his activism alone will force a different result. Rising up like a Miltonic Satan, he recklessly insists that he can win his battle with time. "With something changeless at the heart of me / . . . some nucleus that's myself" (2394-95), he announces he will hold firm until, even in another world, "All that was, is; and must forever be" (2399). Like the speaker of "The Bishop Orders His Tomb" Guido seeks to counteract mutability with protective illusions that deny his actual, present-tense sensations. But his hope that reality will conform to his static fabrications has already been exploded by the Pope, who announces the beginning of a new age, when faith in the report will be replaced by faith in the thing and "Man's God, by God's God" (X. 1874). The time has come, the Pope sees, "to shake / This torpor of assurance from our creed / Re-introduce the doubt discarded" (1853-55).

As Guido is finally led away by the Company of Death, the assured, heroic posture crumbles: "Sirs, my first true word, all truth and no lie, / Is — save me notwithstanding! Life is all!" (2420-21). His "first true word" contradicts none of the meaning implied in his previous words. Guido has no solution to the problem of time. Sheer terror of the passing moment causes him to abandon rhetoric and reveal directly his forlorn, helpless condition. His final utterance is a desperate plea for help, beginning with the Abate and Cardinal, whom he has just rebuked, and ending with Pompilia, the object of his deep and irrevocable hatred.

The meaning of the final line — "Pompilia will you let them murder me?" — has divided readers since the poem's publication. Robert Langbaum, though he recognizes the fear and desperation which provoke this last plea by Guido, says, "The implication is that he dies repentant."[12] The question is whether the instinct for self-preservation is an adequate motive for repentance and whether repentance so defined has any meaning in terms of the poem. Certainly Guido argues for the irrelevance of motives, hoping to demonstrate through intricate illustrations that unbelief will serve as well as belief to make man "play a faithful part" (613). But this is the very dissimulation that has obscured the one truth to which the Pope appeals in his condemnation of both Guido and the entire age. The reader who takes seriously the Pope's claim to Truth, "evolved at the last / Painfully, held tenaciously" (X. 231-32), cannot entertain seriously any claim that Guido is saved through repentance. There is nothing to indicate that Browning here modified his views toward repentance, a subject he regarded with suspicion throughout his poetry. The human self realizes its potential not by seeking a removal of the burden of the past but by accepting full responsibility for its actions in time. Guido, in his two speeches, renounces responsibility for his past actions and, finally, for all that he has just said, reducing himself to a pathetic dependence on Pompilia. If there is disappointment in Guido's collapse because it shatters any image of a heroic arch-villain, there is no justification for transforming this disappointment into the next best thing — Guido's salvation. Browning's ending clearly resists either view.

The monologues of Caponsacchi and Pompilia might be considered the focal point of *The Ring and the Book*, not only because of their placement at the mathematical center of the poem but also because they contain the only first-hand account of the experience which is the subject of all twelve books. Although Caponsacchi is not under the necessity of defending himself and has nothing tangible to gain or lose by addressing the judges, he still senses the extreme urgency of the moment, for the minute in which he is asked to speak is also the minute in which Pompilia is dying. The force of time passing thus lends extra passion to his speech, setting it apart from the composed rhetoric of Guido's preceding monologue. On the one hand, he is bitterly indignant toward the judges for waiting too long to take him seriously and, on the other, he is exasperated that he is powerless to serve Pompilia in the precious few moments remaining. Unlike Guido, who welcomes talking as a means of staying the rapid passage of time, Caponsacchi talks reluctantly, frustrated that his words waste the brief time remaining to Pompilia. In his despair and cynicism he announces that his part is done; he is now ready to remove himself from a society mired in ignorance. Yet there remains the possibility, as his own experience has attested, that truth — instantaneous and intuitive — will be revealed on certain occasions to individuals with the right instincts. Although Caponsacchi's disturbed state of mind indicates that the moment of his speech may be crucial to his own understanding, he insists that the present instant is critical not so much for himself as for the judges, who have yet to see Pompilia's truth and be saved:

> Let me, in heaven's name, use the very snuff
> O' the taper in one last spark shall show truth
> For a moment, show Pompilia who was true!
> Not for her sake, but yours ...
> Be her first prayer then presently for you —
> She has done the good to me ...   (VI. 170-73, 178-79)

Browning's irony is unmistakable in Caponsacchi's disregard of the self-creating moment of his speech and in his announcement that the moment of Pompilia's influence upon him is complete. For Caponsacchi the most important moment is in the past, forming the center of the experience he now relates. Recalling first his early career as a cleric, Caponsacchi draws a

108

self-portrait which has striking resemblances to Guido's. Through the encouragement and example of the Church, both men adopted a complacent, escapist attitude toward time. For this fault, Caponsacchi does not escape the censure of the Pope, who at one point refers to him as "youth prolonged though age was ripe" (X. 1130). Caponsacchi himself acknowledges the wastefulness of his life as a priest and, in describing the Church, calls attention to the same double standard Guido exposes in his monologues. The Church's interest in him is curiously parallel to Guido's early interest in Pompilia as an image to counteract his fear of aging. Caponsacchi was sought simply because his youth would enable the Church "in these latter days" (VI. 291) to present a more attractive appearance to the world. This exploitive attempt by the Church to preserve the past through Caponsacchi's youth and vitality paradoxically produced a sense of stagnation within him. Not until Caponsacchi obeyed the promptings of his heart and acted to rescue Pompilia could he redeem the past and claim any value for his life. His awakening to a dynamic self became possible only when the sight of Pompilia made him take time seriously, forced him to substitute an active readiness for the passive role imposed by the Church. From this point the time problem became a vital concern to him, occasioning the struggle that provides the central drama of his account.

For Caponsacchi, Pompilia is an agent of disclosure, but the temporal meanings she reveals cannot of themselves release him from an atemporal fixity. When he sees her at the theater, where she is in attendance with Guido, the lingering effect of her gaze merely aggravates his dissatisfaction, reminding him of his unfitness. She may be in "need of a finger's help" (497), but he finds himself powerless even to reach out to her. When letters arrive, supposedly written by Pompilia and soliciting his help, he senses trickery by Guido and for a month remains immovable. At last he proceeds to Guido's house in a spirit of indignation but is checked by the appearance of Pompilia, who suggests that he must recover his "sound self," "grow healthy now" (753), if she might just be permitted to state her case. Her comparison of her life to a strange dream, curable only if Caponsacchi will awaken her, does indeed resonate within Caponsacchi, newly alerted to his task as Pompilia adds, " ' . . . now the dream goes to involve yourself' " (862). Caponsacchi must act to save both Pompilia and himself from the void that threatens them equally. No longer may he regard time passively; the moment has become critical. Pompilia does not even wait for Caponsacchi's consent — only for an announcement of the time of his coming: " 'To Rome then, — when is it you take me there? / Each minute lost is mortal. When? — I ask' " (879-80). And Caponsacchi's answer is unhesitating: " 'It shall be when it can be' " (881). The spontaneity of his response, made without the deliberations of the intellect, affords to Caponsacchi an awareness which his rational faculty had previously denied him:

> "Thought?" nay, Sirs, what shall follow was not thought;
> I have thought sometimes, and thought long and hard.
>   ... but no such faculty helped here.   (936-37, 944)
>
> In rushed new things, the old were rapt away . . .   (948)
>
> Into another state, under new rule
> I knew myself was passing swift and sure . . .   (964-65)

Caponsacchi's intuition affords him access to a dynamic new reality, as he begins to realize the transformation predicted by Pompilia. The Church, which would "freeze" him to its "heart of stone" (979-80), now seems to hold an inferior claim to the passionate one made by Pompilia, whose "first authoritative word" is "God's" (1013). But as the appointed time approaches — twenty-four hours from their point of meeting — the deep, intuitive forces which had begun to stir within him are immobilized by rational considerations that again leave him a helpless victim of chronological time: " . . . Dawn broke, noon broadened, I — / I sat stone-still, let time run over me" (1022-23). Aware that Pompilia "counts the minutes" (1028, 1042), Caponsacchi nevertheless rationalizes away the necessity of going to her, assuring himself that in entrusting all to God's providence he has followed the course of wisdom.

Caponsacchi returns to Pompilia to offer consolation, but once more the sight of her causes him to put aside his original intention and to take time seriously. She repeats her earlier request — " ' . . . there is time / And one day more: shall I be saved or no?' " (1072-73) — and Caponsacchi once more gives immediate, spontaneous assent. This time the critical moment will not escape him. Trusting intuition solely, he no longer experiences time as an oppressive weight; instead he now is able to persevere toward the moment which holds his deliverance:

> And thus
> Through each familiar hindrance of the day
> Did I make steadily for its hour and end, —
> Felt time's old barrier-growth of right and fit
> Give way through all its twines, and let me go.   (1124-28)

A crescendoing stream of light and sound culminates in "the ecstatic minute" (1138) when Pompilia's radiant soul penetrates the surrounding darkness. The renewal of the life-giving current will occur the instant Caponsacchi joins himself with its motion. In a "tick of time" (1150) the Pope's "athlete on the instant" (X. 1141) leaps into the carriage and the flight is under way.

The flight itself, as Caponsacchi describes it, is not a desperate battle against time but a "true thing" (1168), scarcely accessible to the static modes of the intellect, which can only partially illuminate "the rush and roll of the abyss" (1173) and which do so artificially by separating "Wavelet from wavelet" (1175). Both travelers lose, therefore, the sense of the actual time elapsing during the trip. At one point Caponsacchi tells Pompilia that it has been years since they left Arezzo, and Pompilia in turn hopes that their journey will endure endlessly: "It is the interruption that I dread..." (1313). Gradually, however, the nearness of Rome and Pompilia's weakening physical condition cause the travelers to be increasingly aware of external time, until the interruption feared by Pompilia occurs. The minute, which had formerly permitted Caponsacchi to become joined with a creative, purposeful motion, now intrudes, bringing an abrupt halt to all further progress. It is at the "last minute" (1431) that Caponsacchi, preparing to awaken Pompilia for the few remaining miles of their trip, comes face to face with Count Guido. The confrontation is another of Caponsacchi's critical moments. His heart bids him to rid creation of its chief "miscreate" (1478), but his intellect instead produces inertness, rendering him no more effectual than the cold and impassive representatives of law:

> And while I mused,
> The minute, oh the misery, was gone!
> On either idle hand of me there stood
> Really an officer, nor laughed i' the least:
> Nay, rendered justice to reason, laid
> Logic to heart, as 't were submitted them
> "Twice two makes four." (1498-1504)

For allowing this moment to slip by, Caponsacchi cannot forgive himself; somewhat later he again dwells on it, suggesting that it incriminates him for Pompilia's death:

> I had him one whole moment, as I said —
> As I remember, as will never out
> O' the thoughts of me, — I had him in arm's reach
> There, — as you stand, Sir, now you cease to sit, —
> I could have killed ere he killed his wife,
> And did not: he went off alive and well
> And then effected this last feat — through me! (1890-96)

His attitude separates him further from Guido, who until the end refuses to acknowledge ultimate responsibility for his actions. While Guido could insist

111

that he did not make himself but was a product of the Church's corrupt example, Caponsacchi may offer no excuses. He has in a glance descried his whole self and now views his highest duty as "daring try be good and true" to that self, leaving behind him "the show of things" (1819-20). The challenge of maintaining this vision, now that he is deprived of Pompilia's living example and beset by the dead forms of religion and law, has become at once excruciatingly difficult and yet all the more essential. Having grasped his real self in its flowing through time and having thus discovered the dynamic, spiritual value within the temporal, Caponsacchi must somehow retain enough light to instruct humankind in its moral-spiritual growth:

> To live, and see her learn, and learn by her,
> Out of the low obscure and petty world —
> Or only see one purpose and one will
> Evolve themselves i' the world, change wrong to right . . .
>   (2085-88)

But the vision suddenly proves no more than "a minute's dream" (2097), and Caponsacchi is thrown back fully upon his own resources, faced with returning to a meaningless existence. His glimpse of the luminous, dynamic whole is Browning's ironic equivalent of Kurtz's peering into the dark and dead center of things. The beatific vision proves more merciful than the horrific, however, for Caponsacchi, like Marlowe, returns to the old way of life, impatient with all its pretense and illusion, even as it provokes his testimonial narrative. Thus, in the closing moments of his speech Caponsacchi descends from the heroic role of St. George to the more human one of Everyman. With his final utterance, pathos counterbalances the former grandeur; the ambiguity of human experience is left undisturbed: "O great, just, good God! Miserable me!" Browning leaves it an open question whether the Caponsacchis of the world, facing disappointment and defeat, will retire in solitary contemplation and self-pity or whether, by diligently seeking out new Pompilias, they will perform the act which renews and transforms human existence.

Unaware of Caponsacchi's pessimistic, despairing attitude Pompilia sees no need of explaining her feelings to him: "What I see, oh, he sees and so much more" (VII. 1805). Since death cannot diminish for her the illuminating vision gained through Caponsacchi, the moment of her speech does not appear to be crucial to her understanding. Nonetheless, while "time flies" (37), she is conscious of two priorities: she must leave a true picture of herself for the sake of her son and she must do all in her power to clear the name of Caponsacchi, whose role as spiritual father enables her to over-

112

look the transgression upon her past life by the natural parent. Gaetano, it becomes clear, is a symbol of the new life made possible by Caponsacchi, and half way through her speech she lays the child aside in order to expend her last breath in defense of her heroic savior.

Caponsacchi's significance for Pompilia is that he has rescued her from the void of her existence with Guido and helped restore her to life. Pompilia had been unable to cope with the evil of Guido; instead, she repressed it. Most critics tend to read Pompilia as a static character and her monologue as a continuation of the defensive mechanism she employs to deal with the pain of her experience.[13] Given her innocent purity, bewilderment and vulnerability, she would seem to require dream and illusion to sustain her in the face of an overwhelming, incomprehensible evil. Yet such repression, or blankness, as Pompilia herself comes to see, "is the note of evil: for good lasts" (595). Looking upon most of her life as "death or dream" (605) Pompilia finds that she is saved from non-existence solely by Caponsacchi and the promise of new birth which he brings. Unlike Guido and Caponsacchi, who are both in danger of being frozen in the past, Pompilia is threatened because she has lost all sense of the past. She lives completely out of time, and she cannot awaken from her "terrific dream" (585) until she has been placed back in time. This has been accomplished, she believes, through Caponsacchi's act preserving the small life she carries within her, the temporal "fact" (1748) which rejoins her to the continuity of the larger life:

> I have my support again,
> Again the knowledge that my babe was, is,
> Will be mine only. (895-97)

But Pompilia's awakening in time cannot be complete until she establishes the continuity of her own experience in time, an effort demanding recognition of the past. Thus by bringing "back reluctantly to mind" (633) her married life with Guido, Pompilia acts even in her dying moment to recover her true self in time. The moment is crucial, then, not just to Gaetano and Caponsacchi but especially to herself, for in the very course of her speech she has furthered the task Caponsacchi had enabled her to begin:

> . . . I could lie in such peace and learn so much —
> Begin the task, I see how needful now,
> Of understanding somewhat of my past, —
> Know life a little, I should leave so soon. (1663-66)

Pompilia's absorption in her son early in her monologue permits her to put the recent past temporarily out of her mind. Even her choice of the name, "Gaetano," reflects her concern only with the present and future:

> . . . no old name
> For sorrow's sake; I looked up to the sky
> And took a new saint to begin anew.   (101-03)

At the back of her mind, however, is the troubling thought that Gaetano will some day learn of her past. Against this eventuality she may offer only a mother's vain wish that perhaps her own repression of the past will somehow cause it to become unreal for her son:

> . . . I hope he will regard
> The history of me as what someone dreamed,
> And get to disbelieve it at the last:
> Since to myself it dwindles fast to that,
> Sheer dreaming and impossibility . . .   (108-12)

Pompilia soon discovers, however, that once the past loses its hold, the present and future likewise withdraw into timeless unreality:

> Thus, all my life, —
> As well what was, as what, like this, was not, —
> Looks old, fantastic and impossible:
> I touch a fairy thing that fades and fades.
> — Even to my babe!   (198-202)

Paradoxically her repressive tendencies on her son's behalf threaten her with his loss, for the dream she had hoped would protect him from the past expands "Till even he withdraws into a dream / As the rest do" (213-14).

Pompilia's dreaming stems from a severe crisis of identity. Even before being given to Guido by Violante, she could regard herself as the "unnecessary life" (297), since she was the accidental, unwanted offspring of a prostitute and a stranger. Consequently she has no difficulty finding a motive which will excuse Violante, who saw in Guido a godsend for her daughter. Pompilia's subsequent experience with Guido, however, makes her more determined than ever to be fully "purged of the past" (352) and causes her to anticipate death as a time of amelioration, a time when "past is past" (359). But just as she is able to declare all "one blank" (584), Don Celestine comes upon her, imploring her "For [her] soul's sake, remember what is past, / The better to forgive it" (597-98).

Reluctantly she begins to bring back the four years with Guido, but not with the result expected by Celestine. Maintaining that a supernatural light illuminates the past, Pompilia finds "but little to forgive at last" (637). The motives of Guido as well as Violante seem understandable to her and consequently she cannot blame the actions of either one. Clearly the real villain in Pompilia's world is not any particular individual; what threatens her

114

most — even when she would repress it — is the past itself. The archbishop to whom she appealed for help merely pressed upon her the old custom equating the husband with God. Guido, by his own admission, had based his domination of her upon the fixed authority of law, and moreover associated law with "nature — which is God." Even Celestine's interest in Pompilia's "soul," a concern which would have her retrace to erase her experience, stems from moribund theological dogma and the church's ignorance of the potential of the human self. Pompilia's greatness, the Pope makes clear, is due to her freedom from such anachronisms:

> Thou didst . . . how shall I say? . . . receive so long
> The standing ordinance of God on earth,
> What wonder if the novel claim had clashed
> With old requirement, seemed to supersede
> Too much the customary law? But, brave,
> Thou at first prompting of what I call God,
> And fools call Nature, didst hear, comprehend,
> Accept the obligation laid on thee . . .   (X. 1068-75)

As a result of her brave, intuitive response Pompilia is able finally to "rise from law to law, / The old to new" (X. 1056-57). Yet, because men's distortions of the past have brought her so much suffering, Pompilia tends to undervalue the past — even as she relates it in her monologue. Until she is able to understand her past, the sense of her actual identity will continue to elude her.

As Pompilia directs her attention to the defense of Caponsacchi, the past, which she has recalled incompletely and only with reluctance, begins to come freely to mind. From her very first glimpse of Caponsacchi, Pompilia sees the "glory of his nature" (921), but she can make others see it only by contrasting it to the darker natures that have oppressed her. The urgency of this task convinces her that she must squarely confront her past, withholding none of it: "Since I say anything, say all if true" (1192). And in the very act of recovering the old she uncovers the new:

>   . . . so
> Do new stars bud while I but search for old,
> And fill all gaps i' the glory, and grow him —
> Him I now see make the shine everywhere.   (1567-70)[14]

Having seen the blazing light of Caponsacchi, Pompilia can now fully descry the evil of her husband, whom she characterizes as "dreadful" (1585), "master by hell's right" (1586), and "the serpent" (1589). When he blocks her path to Rome, threatening to freeze her in the past, she can say that she did for once see and do the right thing:

115

> I did spring up, attempt to thrust aside
> That ice-block 'twixt the sun and me, lay low
> The neutralizer of all good and truth.   (1594-96)

The leaping active verbs as well as the lunging action they describe reveal the potential to which the Pope will allude. Brandishing sword against her husband, Pompilia by her action lends credibility to Caponsacchi's insistence that it is she who is the rescuer. Moreover, her aggressive verbal expression, a close and unpremeditated fitting of feelings to words, discloses the transformation she experiences even as she speaks.

Confirmation of Pompilia's new awareness comes as she focuses on the earlier trial and sees that the judges, who decided to sentence her to the convent rather than force her back to Guido, made the right decision. While there, she could begin to seek to understand her past, a task she can "see how needful now" (1664). Moreover, there is evidence that through her present defense of Caponsacchi she has, to a great extent, accomplished this task:

> . . . because this man restored my soul,
> All has been right; I have gained my gain, enjoyed
> As well as suffered . . .   (1667-69)

Whereas Pompilia had previously insisted that her past was necessarily blank because only good endures, she now sees that the whole of the past — both its good and its bad moments — is vital to the creation of self. For this reason Pompilia reaffirms her intention not to pardon Guido; nothing is gained by remembering the past for the sake of absolving it. But what she does remember she will turn to good account. No longer will she fear Guido and attempt to repress him within her consciousness:

> Whatever he touched is rightly ruined: plague
> It caught, and disinfection it had craved
> Still but for Guido; I am saved through him
> So as by fire; to him — thanks and farewell!   (1736-39)

Guido's malignity is no less responsible than Caponsacchi's heroics for the self-identity she only now begins to realize. Having discovered that in human experience the means are ultimately justified by the end, Pompilia may confidently say that "[God] will explain in time" (1760) all that she is now incapable of expressing. Caponsacchi requires no such explanation, she believes, for he already sees more than she does; he must know that they will be united "when the true time is" (1837). It is clear to Pompilia that "true time" cannot be separated from human experience, for she and Caponsacchi had already glimpsed such a time during the course of their flight. But even more significant to Pompilia than the moment of the flight is the present — "this supreme of moments" (1821). Her life, which only moments before had seemed like a dark, insupportable nightmare, is now radiant with meaning and purpose. Because of her triumph — the recovery of her true self in its evolving life in time — Pompilia offers humanity her highest consolation in the form of a challenge:

> Could we by a wish
> Have what we will and get the future now,
> Would we wish aught done undone in the past?
> So, let him wait God's instant men call years . . . (1838-41)

Unknown to Pompilia, her earthly saint even now submits to what he considers a past failure, a failure which makes the "true, / The good, the eternal" (VI. 2089-90) seem hopelessly "far away" (2096). Caponsacchi's despair is intensified by his sense of a remote, distant God who chooses never to stoop. But perhaps Pompilia's final words — praise of God's justice from one who apparently has least cause to praise — will, in time, penetrate the doubt:

> Through such souls alone
> God stooping shows sufficient of His light
> For us i' the dark to rise by. And I rise.   (1843-45)

117

Conclusion: Fact and Fancy

> ... somehow fact
> Has got to — say, not so much push aside
> Fancy, as to declare its place supplied
> By fact unseen but no less fact the same ...
>
> ("Gerard de Lairesse," 149-52)

The distinction between fact and fancy is a major theme throughout Browning's poetry, from *Pauline* to his last work, a collection subtitled *Fancies and Facts*. Nowhere has Browning provoked more controversy than in his understanding and use of historical fact in *The Ring*. Because of obvious discrepancies between the Yellow Book and the poem, numerous commentators have been disturbed by Browning's insistence that he has merely presented "fact untampered with."[1] The poem apparently bears too many traces of imaginative license to support Browning's claim that the alloy of his imagination had merely a shaping, rather than a constitutive, role in the final form, which Browning likens to a ring composed of pure gold, or fact. But incredulity over the ring metaphor results only when we insist on identifying the poet's understanding of fact with our own literal definition of the term. If we follow the example of the poet and fuse our souls with the documental material — "that inert stuff" (I. 469) — we should perceive much more than the isolated events recorded by human intellect. Yet what we sympathetically apprehend — a changing, living process — will be no less real than fact itself. A separation of fact from truth would suggest a false dichotomy between finite and infinite, an appeal from a mutable world of human experience to an absolute, transcendental order. Since Browning wishes to squeeze directly from the facts their true values, he must take all precautions against sacrificing the facts which serve as the basis of his poem.

It is best, then, to admit that Browning's fidelity to historical fact, as we commonly understand the term "fact," falls far short of our usual requirements for accurate reporting of the past. This acknowledged, we may be receptive to the possibility that Browning's poetic re-creations are indeed faithful to fact as *he* understands the term, or wishes it to be understood. Through the major characters' references to fact, we can see that Browning himself is aware of two possible interpretations and that only one is finally valid.

Both Guido and Caponsacchi hold a double awareness of fact, which produces opportunism in one and revulsion in the other. Guido knows that law closely identifies itself with fact; in his first speech he exploits this presumption by reminding the judges of their earlier verdict:

> Law has pronounced there's punishment, less or more:
> And I take note o' the fact and use it thus —
> For the first flaw in the original bond,
> I claim release.   (V. 1293-96)

However, in his second speech, with nothing to win or lose, Guido candidly states that fact has lost its meaning and become subject to human distortions — "feigning everywhere grows fact" (XI. 589). To support this statement Guido challenges the Church to muster up more than a small fraction of its members who could "Prove their faith a fact so far" (701).

Caponsacchi, too, sees that the court's high regard for fact is a pretense, or justice might have been done at the first trial. With indignant sarcasm he prods the judges with their favorite word. Despite their claim to have "knowledge of the facts" (VI. 1682), they are too obtuse to see the one fact that "seems to fill the universe with sight and sound" (66-67). Caponsacchi sees, much to his exasperation, that the lesson which he and Pompilia learned "from the first o' the fact" (80) has made no more impression on the judges than it did on the authorities who could have helped Pompilia. The only fact that can be applied to law and Church, he demonstrates, is that both feign fact. Pompilia's appeal to the Governor and the Archbishop had fallen upon deaf ears; thus she had "tried and proved the fact" (826) of their simulation. Caponsacchi, on the other hand, responded to Pompilia's appeal; by rejecting the influence of law and Church and obeying instead an internal impulse, he immediately recognized fact:

> Pompilia spoke, and I at once received,
> Accepted my own fact, my miracle
> Self-authorized and self-explained . . .   (918-20)

With this dependence upon an inner light, Caponsacchi is able to reduce his defense to one fact, the only appeasement he will offer his judges:

> That I assuredly did bow, was blessed
> By the revelation of Pompilia. There!
> Such is the final fact I fling you, Sirs,
> To mouth and mumble and misinterpret: there!   (1859-61)

119

The Pope likewise has but one fact to offer to skeptics and unbelievers:

> This I refer still to the foremost fact,
> Life is probation and the earth no goal
> But starting-point of man: compel him strive,
> Which means, in man, as good as reach the goal . . .
> (X. 1435-38)

The greatest threat to belief, then, is closure; any fact which represents experience as a completed act is less than factual, or, as Caponsacchi puts it, fact "lower set i' the scale" (VI. 69). To Caponsacchi, Pompilia, and the Pope the foremost fact is the human capacity for unending development, for ceaseless becoming. As Pompilia approaches death, "the fact that means so much" (VII. 1748) is not her release from a sordid existence but her growth in self-knowledge as she realizes her continuity with the past through her son Gaetano and her importance to the present in defending Caponsacchi.

Through the significant characters of the poem, then, Browning seeks to redefine fact by exposing the discrepancies between its conventional and actual meaning. The distinction is one carefully explained by Bergson: "That which is commonly called *fact* is not reality as it appears to immediate intuition, but an adaptation of the real to the interests of practice and to the exigencies of social life. Pure intuition, external or internal, is that of an undivided continuity. We break up this continuity into elements laid side by side, which correspond in the one case to distinct *words*, in the other to independent objects."[2] Browning exposes the real fact, the "undivided continuity," by opposing the clear-sighted, intuitive perceptions of Caponsacchi and Pompilia to the environmentally conditioned, habitual responses of the public. But Browning has yet a great problem — how to make the reader *feel* the continuity which is contradicted in the very act of being broken up into words. The answer is to be found not in the static conceptualizations of the historian but in the imaginative re-creations of the artist:

> . . . Art, — wherein man nowise speaks to men,
> Only to mankind, — Art may tell a truth
> Obliquely, do the thing shall breed the thought,
> Nor wrong the thought, missing the mediate word.
> (XII. 858-6)

Rather than sacrifice fact, art alone is capable of saving the facts by at once recognizing the inadequacy of mediate linguistic signs, literal or figurative, to represent stable, self-authenticating knowledge and by emphasizing the creative act which brings the dynamic reality fully into play. Since the poet

120

knows that the form he has chosen is the "one way possible / Of speaking truth" (XII. 843-44), he will not accept any suggestion that he has presented less than the facts. He has simply re-established their continuity with all human experience, including the reader's, by restoring to them their original mobility:

> Red, green and blue that whirl into a white,
> The variance now, the eventual unity,
> Which make the miracle. See it for yourselves,
> This man's act, changeable because alive!   (I. 1362-65)

The opposition between fancy and fact remains a thematic preoccupation with the poet until his death. The artist's only concern, Browning would always insist, is with facts; fancy is simply an instrument employed to reveal their real flux and continuity. Because "time means amelioration, tardily enough displayed, / Yet a mainly onward moving, never wholly retrograde" (*La Saisiaz*, 415-16), the poet, in presenting facts, is able to reveal "the old things thus made new" ("Christopher Smart," 148). It follows that art must be subservient to facts. Art is not a thing in itself but a symbol of the temporal values which constitute reality:

> Art is my evidence
> That something was, is, might be; but no more thing
> Than Flame is fuel.   (*Fifine at the Fair*, 1524-27)

The opposition between fancy and fact is a source of productive tension in the poems in which it has an implicit, dramatic function. In the later poetry, as the theme comes increasingly to the surface, the poet's insistence on the validity of the artist's imagination paradoxically has a devitalizing influence on his own art. Yet Browning's dramatization and resolution of this conflict are crucial to an understanding of his development and originality as a poet. Pauline's lover and Paracelsus are both closely identified with the poet's viewpoint, expressing intense frustration and disillusionment over their inability to reconcile a lofty idealism with the hard facts of existence. Paracelsus, however, finally achieves the realization that despite the failure of his grandiose aspirations, self and nature are allied to a common value through the dynamic, creative movement of time. Sordello is another idealistic hero whose fancies remove him from the facts of a temporal world. But Browning has by now increased aesthetic distance from his hero sufficiently to portray more critically and dramatically the conflict expressed in the previous two poems. Next, in the most representative dramatic monologues Browning gives new focus to the theme, compressing it into a single moment which is at once the content and structure of the poem. The influence of time in these poems upon an inner consciousness caught between the claims of fancy and fact, intellect and intuition, suggests the special, psychological understanding of time which Bergsonian duration affords. Finally, in *The Ring and the Book* Browning takes the raw, pure facts and arranges them in an elaborate, symphonic pattern — exposition, development, recapitulation — to illustrate for the reader their life and meaning. Through Pompilia, who rejects dreaming and unifies all the facts of her experience within one supreme moment, Browning achieves perhaps his noblest utterance on the theme which is, literally, the driving force behind his poetry.

For Browning the self lives in time, and not in space. The greatest challenge is always

> 'From the given point evolve the infinite!'
> Not — 'Spend thyself in space, endeavoring to joint
> Together, and so make infinite, point and point. . . . '
> (*Fifine*, 2295-97)

The attempt to view reality rationally as a collection of inert external points in space is a misguided application of human energies. Rather than tackle the world from the outside, human beings must intuitively grasp the living, inner reality of immediate experience. Only then does an individual discover that life's essence is ceaseless becoming: each moment is seen to express this movement, and the self in turn is viewed as the center of free and creative action.

Browning's feeling for time leaves no room whatsoever for any of the popular nineteenth-century views associating evolution with a naturalistic, mechanical process, as can be found, for example, in the hypotheses of Darwin and the philosophy of Herbert Spencer. Nor can he be closely identified with any of the abstract, intellectualized conceptions of process advanced by nineteenth-century idealists. For Browning speculative notions about the immanent workings of an absolute spirit are beside the point. The realization of self and the direct experience of a spiritual life in the concrete facts of existence are always his foremost concerns as a poet. He rejects equally cause-effect and deterministic explanations of reality. Instead, the flow of experience reveals "a force / Actual ere its own beginning, operative through its course, / Unaffected by its end" (*La Saisiaz*, 219-21).

It is unfortunate and quite remarkable, then, if Browning's reputation should bear any scars from the attacks once leveled at him by Henry Jones and Santayana. Jones, as a neo-Hegelian convinced that rational inquiry would reveal an immanent and unified spiritual reality,[3] could not possibly have been sympathetic towards Browning's view of knowledge. And it is

122

hardly surprising that Santayana, whose method is rational and whose view of nature is frankly materialist and mechanistic,[4] should have considered Browning's art primitive and barbaric. Browning's philosophic kinship is with the vitalism of Bergson and the pragmaticism of William James[5] — philosophies which recognize the severe limitations of intellect and stress the primacy of action. Finally, the concerns in Browning's poetry — with inner consciousness, self and freedom — are strongly suggestive of much existentialist thought. In line with most existentialist philosophers, moreover, Browning views perception as an active encounter of a real perceiver with a real object. There is no split between mind and matter; human perception is of the real world.[6]

And here we are brought back to the subject of time, for where the existentialist perceives a fragmented world of threat and anxiety, Browning experiences a dynamic, purposeful world of ceaseless becoming. Whereas the view from above, as the poet emphasizes in his 1887 poem, "Parleying With Francis Furini," reveals an abyss of darkness and ignorance, the prospect from below is far more luminous. Rather than despair of influencing the succession of events in time, the creative artist derives his strength from the knowledge that he *is* time.

> 'Enough that now,
> Here where I stand, this moment's me and mine
> Shows me what is, permits me to divine
> What shall be.'   ("Francis Furini," 420-23)

NOTES

INTRODUCTION

¹ (Glasgow, 1891; Philadelphia: R. West, 1973).

² "The Poetry of Barbarism," rpt. in *The Browning Critics,* ed. Boyd Litzinger and K. L. Knickerbocker (Lexington: University of Kentucky Press, 1965).

³ See, e.g., William Raymond, *The Infinite Moment,* 2nd ed. (Toronto: University of Toronto Press, 1965) and E. D. H. Johnson, *The Alien Vision of Victorian Poetry* (Princeton: Princeton University Press, 1952).

⁴ See, e.g., Dallas Kenmare, *An End to Darkness* (London: P. Owen, 1962) and Norton Crowell, *The Triple Soul* (Albuquerque: University of New Mexico Press, 1963).

⁵ *The Poetry of Experience* (New York: Norton, 1957) and *The Disappearance of God* (Cambridge, Mass.: Harvard University Press, 1963).

⁶ *Ringers in the Tower* (Chicago: University of Chicago Press, 1971); *The Anxiety of Influence* (New York: Oxford University Press, 1973); *A Map of Misreading* (New York: Oxford University Press, 1975); *Poetry and Repression* (New Haven: Yale University Press, 1976).

⁷ *Movements of Thought in the Nineteenth Century* (Chicago: University of Chicago, 1936) and *Studies in Human Time,* Elliott Coleman, trans. (Baltimore: Johns Hopkins Press, 1956).

⁸ *Movements of Thought in the Nineteenth Century,* pp. xv ff., 35 ff., 66 ff. Humean scepticism, it should be noted, has found a modern day analogue in deconstructionist criticism, which also challenges the assumptions implicit in the concept of "self."

⁹ (Cambridge, Mass.: Harvard, 1966).

¹⁰ (London: Ernest Benn, 1931).

¹¹ In *Victorian Poetry,* Malcolm Bradbury and David Palmer, eds. (London: Edward Arnold, 1972), pp. 58-87.

¹² (Toronto: University of Toronto, 1963).

¹³ (Minneapolis, Minn.: University of Minnesota Press, 1980), p. 6.

¹⁴ Much the same question is raised by Clyde de L. Ryals' *Becoming Browning: The Poems and Plays of Robert Browning: 1833-1846* (Columbus: Ohio State University Press, 1983), which arrived as the present manu-

script was going to press. Ryals' focus is not so much on time as on the implications of non-teleological becoming for the ironic theory and practice of the poet. Drawing heavily upon Friedrich Schlegel, Ryals sees Browning as a Romantic Ironist, continually hovering between being and becoming, finite and infinite, form and content, self-creation and self-negation. In tracing Browning's development as an ironist, Ryals investigates the plays, though he (wisely) does not attempt to revise the estimate of them as unplayable artifacts.

¹⁵ (Athens, Ohio: Ohio University Press, 1982).

¹⁶ (Totowa, New Jersey: Barnes and Noble, 1982).

CHAPTER I

¹ Samuel Alexander, *Space, Time and Deity* (London: Macmillan, 1934), I, 44.

² See Georges Poulet, *Studies in Human Time*, pp. 34-35.

³ *The Triumph of Time*, p. 8.

⁴ See Christopher Salveson, *The Landscape of Memory* (Lincoln, Nebr.: University of Nebraska Press, 1965), pp. 2-3.

⁵ *Time and Free Will*, trans. F. L. Pogson (1910; rpt. New York: Harper and Row, 1960), p. 90.

⁶ *Time and Free Will*, p. 98.

⁷ *Creative Evolution*, trans. Arthur Mitchell (1913; rpt. Westport, Conn.: Greenwood Press, 1975), p. 4.

⁸ *Creative Evolution*, p. 4.

⁹ *Matter and Memory*, trans. Nancy Margaret Paul and W. Scott Palmer (London: George Allen, 1911), p. 194.

¹⁰ *Matter and Memory*, p. 232.

¹¹ *Matter and Memory*, p. 171. Shiv Kumar, in *Bergson and the Stream of Consciousness Novel* (New York: New York University Press, 1963), quite arbitrarily applies Proust's distinction between *mémoire involuntaire* and *mémoire voluntaire* to Bergson's distinction between two forms of memory. However, whereas Proust asserts the supremacy of the first, Bergson emphasizes the complementary activities of the two. The spontaneous, recollective memory provides the active, forward moving memory with images so as to guide its choice (*Matter and Memory*, pp. 98 f.). Poulet, in *Studies in Human Time*, says "nothing is more false than to compare Proustian duration with Bergsonian duration" (p. 316). Proustian existence is a retrospective one; not a unity advancing in time (p. 320). The point I wish to bring out is that Bergsonian duration is especially consonant with the nineteenth century view of time as perpetual progress, as creative becoming.

[12] "Philosophical Intuition," in *The Creative Mind,* trans. Mabelle L. Andison (New York, 1946), pp. 151-52.

[13] *Introduction to Metaphysics,* trans. T. E. Hulme (New York: Putnam, 1912), p. 7.

[14] *Creative Evolution,* pp. 267, 268.

[15] Robert Browning, *The Works of Robert Browning,* ed. F. G. Kenyon (London, 1912). With the exception of Chapter II, all citations from Browning's poetry in my text are to this edition.

[16] Matthew Arnold, *The Poetical Works of Matthew Arnold,* ed. C. B. Tinker and H. F. Lowry (London, 1950).

[17] Alfred Tennyson, *Poetical Works* (London: Oxford, 1953).

[18] Quoted in William DeVane, *A Browning Handbook* (New York: Appleton-Century-Crofts, 1955), p. 229.

[19] *The Poetry of Experience,* p. 195.

[20] *The Poetry of Experience,* p. 199.

[21] For a review of the diversity of interpretations the poem has received, see Ian Jack, *Browning's Major Poetry* (London: Oxford University Press, 1973), pp. 179-80.

[22] *The Ringers in the Tower,* p. 162.

[23] DeVane, "The Landscape of 'Childe Roland,' " *PMLA,* XL (1925), 427.

[24] *The Anxiety of Influence,* p. 130; *A Map of Misreading,* pp. 106, 111-22; *Poetry and Repression,* pp. 199-201. See, also, Constance Hassett, *The Elusive Self in the Poetry of Robert Browning*: "By confronting the spectre of ultimate meaninglessness, Roland establishes his essential autonomy" (p. 112); and, for a related but more pessimistic recent view, see E. Warwick Slinn, *Browning and the Fictions of Identity*: "Roland is caught within his own quest...and all he can discover through the awareness of this trap is his own end, for only in the fire of transformation is there release from consciousness and such a release is synonymous with death" (p. 162).

[25] Browning frequently pictures even a heaven of progress. Eternity is envisioned not as the absence of time but as unending time, an opportunity for further development in the life after death.

[26] *The Poetry of Experience,* p. 199.

[27] *Time and Free Will,* p. 126.

[28] *The Poetry of Experience,* pp. 197, 198.

[29] *Time and Free Will,* p. 231.

CHAPTER II

[1] From a letter to Ruskin, published in *The Works of John Ruskin,* ed. E. T. Cook and Alexander Wedderburn, vol. 36 (London: Allen, 1909), p. xxxiv.

² *The Complete Works of Robert Browning*, ed. Roma A. King, Jr., et al. (Athens, Ohio, 1969-   ). In Chapter II all citations from Browning's poetry in my text are to this edition.

³ Introductory note to the 1868 edition.

⁴ See R. D. Laing, *The Divided Self* (New York: Pelican, 1965), pp. 69-77.

⁵ John Stuart Mill's remarks are certainly right to the point: "The self-seeking and self-worshipping state is well described — beyond that, I should think the writer had made, as yet, only the next step, viz. into despising his own state; he does not write as if it were purged out of him." Printed in W. Hall Griffin and Harry Christopher Minchin, *The Life of Robert Browning*, 3rd ed. (1938; rpt. Hamden, Connecticut: Archon Books, 1966), p. 59.

⁶ Pauline's role in the poem is closely examined by Park Honan, in *Browning's Characters: A Study in Poetic Technique* (New Haven, 1961). Her function, according to Honan, is two-fold: she motivates the speaker's self-revelations and is herself a part of his spiritual dilemma. "Through Pauline, Browning's poet-hero becomes not only a narrator of past events, but a dramatic figure of the present, struggling with the very real and immediate problem of human love as represented by the woman to whom he addresses himself" (p. 16). In some respects, this seems to me an over-statment. While Pauline does provide an excuse for the speaker's confession, she is not sufficiently realized as a character, or even as a human being, to be taken seriously as a dramatic force in the poem. The speaker's love, as I try to show, is something far less than "real and immediate," because it is scornful of the past and removed from temporal existence. As Mill was quick to observe: "I should think it a sincere confession, though of a most unlovable state, if the 'Pauline' were not evidently a mere phantom.... I know not what to wish for him but that he may meet a *real* Pauline" (Griffin and Minchin, p. 59).

⁷ See, esp., Frederick A. Pottle, *Shelley and Browning: A Myth and Some Facts* (Chicago: Pembroke Press, 1923), pp. 34-64, and Tucker, pp. 32-40.

⁸ Quoted in William Irvine and Park Honan, *The Book, The Ring, and the Poet* (New York: McGraw-Hill, 1974), p. 497.

⁹ "Essay on Shelley," *Complete Works*, Vol. V, pp. 149, 151.

¹⁰ Introductory Note to 1868 edition.

¹¹ See, e.g., Constance W. Hassett, *The Elusive Self in the Poetry of Robert Browning*, pp. 8-9; Herbert Tucker, *Browning's Beginnings*, pp. 46-47; and Masao Miyoshi, "Mill and *Pauline*: The Myth and Some Facts," *VS*, IX (December 1965), 154-63. All readings share the tendency to take the speaker at his word, whereas Mill's point is that the speaker's profession of humility, love, and acceptance is a self-deception which should not be taken at face value.

[12] Griffin and Minchin, pp. 59-60.

[13] 1835 edition. Printed in *The Complete Works*, ed. Roma King, et al.

[14] Herbert Tucker, *Browning's Beginnings*, interprets Paracelsus' ability to see the robe instead of the form as an advance in understanding. If language is "the dress of thought," Parcelsus "enjoys a triumph" by seeing how language through memory "can change and renew what he has thought was lost" (pp. 69-70). Paracelsus himself, however, senses no such triumph in II. 156-68, and the implication is that the robe he now sees is not the "wondrous natural robe" (l. 160) he once saw attiring the truth.

[15] "Paracelsus," trans. R. F. C. Hull, in Vol. 15 of *The Collected Works*, ed. Sir Herbert Read, et al. (New York, 1966), pp. 6, 9.

[16] *The Infinite Moment*, 2nd ed., p. 170.

[17] P. 4.

[18] P. 271.

[19] Norton Crowell, *The Triple Soul*, p. 137.

[20] Elvan Kintner, ed., *The Letters of Robert Browning and Elizabeth Barrett 1845-1846* (Cambridge, Mass.: Belknap Press, 1969), I, 26.

[21] Letter of 5 March 1866, in *The Letters of Robert Browning Collected by Thomas J. Wise*, ed. Thurman L. Hood (New Haven, Conn.: Yale University Press, 1933).

[22] *Time and Free Will*, p. 98.

[23] Herbert Tucker, in *Browning's Beginnings*, identifies numerous commentators who have described Browning's method in Sordello as an attempt to achieve the effect of simultaneity (pp. 95, 231). On the accuracy and worth of such descriptions, Tucker's comment is especially noteworthy: "... they impose a critical muzzle on Browning that is useful if only because it represents so clearly what he is laboring in *Sordello* to throw off" (p. 95). In *Sordello* Browning is moving away from the spatialization of time suggested by concepts such as simultaneity to a realization of the dynamic temporal nature of human experience and language.

[24] In the *Essay on Shelley*, Browning characterizes the subjective poet as one who withdraws from the "imperfect exhibitions of nature in the manifold experience of man around him, which serve only to distract and suppress the working of his brain" (*The Complete Works*, V, 139).

[25] *The Divided Self*, pp. 78-82.

[26] *The Sickness Unto Death*, W. Lowrie, trans. (Princeton, N.J.: 1953), p. 169.

[27] *The Complete Works*, V, 139.

[28] *The Divided Self*, p. 88.

[29] For a stimulating discussion on Eglamor's role in the poem and a close, virtuosic analysis of lines 797-819 see Herbert Tucker, *Browning's Beginnings*, pp. 16-29.

[30] Robert Columbus and Claudette Kemper, "Sordello and the Speaker: A Problem in Identity," *VP*, II (Winter, 1964), 251-67. I follow the approach of most critics in closely identifying Browning with the speaker. The speaker's reflections upon the circumstances of the composition of *Sordello* — his trip to Italy when the poem was half completed, etc. — are sufficient evidence to discount the possibility of a distinct persona.

[31] The best introduction to Derrida's thought is *Of Grammatology*, trans. Gayatri Chakravorty Spivak (Baltimore, Md.: Johns Hopkins University Press, 1977).

[32] See W. David Shaw, *The Dialectical Temper* (Ithaca, N.Y.: Cornell University Press, 1968), pp. 34-35, 38. Shaw compounds the difficulties of the passage by ascribing it to Sordello rather than to the narrator.

[33] Browning's removal in the 1888 edition of the clarifying head-notes he had inserted in the 1863 edition is but another indication of the priority he attaches in *Sordello* to the development of a soul — in this case the composer's own.

[34] *Matter and Memory*, p. 171.

[35] Preface to the 1837 edition.

[36] *Robert Browning's Moral-Aesthetic Theory 1833-1855* (Lincoln, Nebraska, 1967), pp. 83, 85.

[37] *The Dialectical Temper*, p. 47.

[38] See, e.g., Tucker, *Browning's Beginnings*: "Constrained by the closural scheme of *Pippa Passes*, Browning's characters hold the undeniable fascination of wind-up dolls cunningly devised to go through the elaborate motions of shutting themselves off. . . . Even at the last minute God's puppets exhibit an independent activity — if only the curious activity of fastening themselves to the divine strings and then hardening into wooden simplicity" (p. 127). For a favorable estimate of the poem's influence on Browning's handling of time see Lawrence Poston, III, "Browning's Career to 1841: The Theme of Time and the Problem of Form," in *Browning Institute Studies, Vol. 3* (New York, 1975), pp. 94-99.

[39] *The Focusing Artifice* (Athens: Ohio University Press, 1968), p. 49.

CHAPTER III

[1] This designation was not a part of common usage until William James called attention to it in *Principles of Psychology* (1890; rpt. New York: Dover, 1950), I, 609.

[2] *Red Cotton Night-Cap Country*, l. 4236.

[3] "By the Fireside," l. 251.

[4] The most useful psychological paradigm for Browning's concept of "self" is not to be found in psychoanalytic theory but in the "humanistic," "Third Force" school grouped around psychologists such as Carl Rogers

and Abraham Maslow. For Rogers, the individual becomes increasingly whole and healthy as he or she overcomes conceptualizations based on past experiences and learns to interpret the present moment in its own immediate terms as constantly changing flow (See, especially, *On Becoming a Person*, Boston, 1961). Maslow concentrates on "self-actualizers" and finds that common to all is the experiencing of certain intense moments, which he calls "peak experiences." In such moments, as in Browning's infinite moments, the individual perceives a wholeness in which past and future are integral with the present moment (See *Toward a Psychology of Being*, New York, 1968).

[5] R. G. Collingwood, *The Idea of History* (New York, 1956), pp. 20-21.

[6] "Browning as Poet of Religion," *Bulletin of the John Rylands Library*, XXVII (1942-1943), 284.

[7] Cleon's envious references to "the natural man" and endorsement of the "lower and inconscious forms of life," though indicative of this growing awareness of the limitations of the intellect, are in no way offered by Browning as the antidote to intellectual pride. Browning's unflattering portrait of Caliban, who represents a regression in human consciousness, should dispel any notion that Browning supports primitivism. Yet Georg Roppen, in *Evolution and Poetic Belief* (Oslo, 1956), wrote "However uncongenial Schopenhauer's pessimistic philosophy was to Browning at this period of his life, his interpretation of the specific human tragedy, of 'man's failure,' in this poem includes such a central idea as the curse of consciousness (p. 130). Henry Duffin, in *Amphibian: A Reconsideration of Browning* (London, 1956), went so far as to scold Browning for having a bad attitude and then offered to the poet a new version of the poem: "The mood of Browning's poem is unnecessarily depressed: I do not know why either the Greek poet in his lily-isle or Browning, recently married and at the age of 43 ... should have been cast down by, or even have known anything about, this decreased recipiency for joy.... The idea that a limitation will be released in death is sounder and more acceptable than the one of compensation" (p. 215). Both statements illustrate the common fallacy in earlier Browning criticism of ignoring the dramatic voice of the poet.

[8] For an indication of how Browning's imagery, syntax, rhythm and phonetic sounds enforce the suggestion of a split in Cleon's personality see Roma King, *The Bow and the Lyre: The Art of Robert Browning* (Ann Arbor: University of Michigan Press, 1957), pp. 194-96, and Park Honan, *Browning's Characters*, p. 249.

[9] See Thomas Collins, *Browning's Moral-Aesthetic Theory*, pp. 93-124.

[10] William Raymond, *The Infinite Moment*, p. 39.

[11] DeVane, *Handbook*, noted that the poem was a favorite of the poet and possibly is "more esteemed than any other" (p. 257).

[12] This important difference of "Saul" from Browning's more characteristic dramatic monologues provides a large basis of the rather strong charge

Roma King, in *The Bow and The Lyre* and again in *The Focusing Artifice*, brings against the poem. King's main criterion for evaluating Browning's monologues is the conflict in character out of which Browning creates artistic unity. In "Saul" the conflict, King feels, is in Browning's artistic intentions and confused structure; it is not a dynamic element of dramatic form. Browning's interest is not clearly focused on either Saul or David and when he speaks in his own voice he shifts attention from the dramatic to the didactic. Partly dramatic, partly lyrical, "Saul" is "brilliant in part but lacks artistic wholeness" (*The Bow and the Lyre*, p. 123). Constance Hassett, in *The Elusive Self*, attempts to meet such objections by placing the emphasis on David's "conversion" and apprehension of "transcendence" (p. 49). But "conversion" is a strong and potentially misleading word to describe David's lyric inspirations, which reveal, moreover, not a transcendent deity but an immanent, incarnate one. The artistic unity of "Saul" is best appreciated when we regard the monologue as a visionary poem of the order of "Abt Vogler." Despite the close identification of poet and speaker, moreover, the poem's resolution is not exactly didactic, for it is presented as a dramatic experience. The strengths of "Saul" suggest we should not judge the poem on the basis of Browning's typical monologues.

[13] *Robert Browning: How to Know Him* (1915; rpt. Norwood, Penn.: Norwood Editions, 1932), p. 140. This quotation invites speculation concerning the extent of Phelps' influence on his most famous pupil, Cole Porter, who certainly made the case for passion as the "motive power" of American life.

[14] *The Browning Cyclopedia* (London, 1897), p. 253.

[15] P. 238.

[16] *An End to Darkness*, p. 148.

[17] *The Triple Soul*, p. 11.

[18] Traditionally critics seem to have taken liberties especially with this poem for the sake of a "fresh interpretation." Irving Orenstein ("A Fresh Interpretation of 'The Last Ride Together'," *Baylor Browning Interests Series*, No. 18, Waco, Texas, 1961; pp. 3-10), prefers to regard the lady as Muse and the poem as "a confession of the poet's own feeling of inadequacy" (p. 3). This reading certainly places a new slant upon the poem, but one that hardly seems to be for the better. If we regard the "dearest" whom the speaker addresses as an abstraction rather than a flesh and blood lady, the poem loses in dramatic immediacy and in the universality of its human experience what it gains in autobiographical interest.

Russell Goldfarb ("Sexual Meaning in 'The Last Ride Together'," *VP*, III [1965], 255-61), bases his interpretation on the "now vulgar coitional meaning of the word 'ride' " (p. 255). The speaker "apparently glimpses heaven at the climax of intercourse" (p. 260), and his vision of the instant made eternity suggests "the climax of the ride prolonged eternally" (p. 256). Goldfarb holds up the line, "Thus lay she a moment on my breast" (33), and suggests we have an awkward picture if we imagine the man and woman sitting on horse-back at this point. He fails, however, to mention that the speaker specifies that the lady and he are "side by side" (19), a no less difficult image if we place the two in the position preferred by Goldfarb.

19 *Robert Browning* (London: Macmillan, 1903), p. 175.

20 William DeVane, in "The Virgin and the Dragon," *Yale Review*, XXXVII (1947), pp. 33-46, said, "Not since John Donne had any such intimate revelation of married love been given us" (p. 40).

21 Duffin, p. 89.

22 W. David Shaw, "Character and Philosophy in 'Fra Lippo Lippi'," *VP*, II (1964), 127-32.

23 *The Poetry of Experience*, pp. 46, 140.

24 Shaw, p. 131.

25 *The Bow and the Lyre*, p. 11.

26 Constance Hassett, *The Elusive Self*, p. 131.

27 Poulet, p. 8.

28 (New York: Doubleday, 1954), p. 244.

29 Poulet, p. 8.

30 For this reason, much of the ongoing critical debate generated by the poem — a controversy over the Duke's precise effect upon his auditor — seems to me wide of the mark.

31 *The Bow and the Lyre*, p. 11.

CHAPTER IV

1 *Notes on Novelists* (London, 1914), p. 306.

2 Richard D. Altick and James F. Loucks, II, *Browning's Roman Murder Story* (Chicago: University of Chicago Press, 1968), pp. 2-3. It should be noted that this statement was made before the appearance of Mary R. Sullivan's solid critical study, *Browning's Voices in "The Ring and the Book"* (Toronto: University of Toronto Press, 1969).

3 Killham, "Browning's Modernity: *The Ring and the Book*, and Relativism," in *The Major Victorian Poets*, ed. Isobel Armstrong (Lincoln, Nebr., 1969), pp. 153-75, and Jack, *Browning's Major Poetry*, pp. 273-99. A different and more recent view is offered by E. Warwick Slinn, who finds that Browning, in *The Ring*, is "more concerned to explore the psychology of authentic action than the theology of moral truth" (*Browning and the Fictions of Identity*, p. 132).

4 *Browning's Roman Murder Story*, p. 2.

[5] P. 35.

[6] P. 227.

[7] William Whitla, in *The Central Truth*, calls *The Ring* a *duration*, an overlapping succession, a number of quasi-simultaneities (p. 121). E. D. H. Johnson in "Robert Browning's Pluralistic Universe: A Reading of *The Ring and the Book*," *University of Toronto Quarterly*, 31 (October 1961), 20-41, finds the best explanation of the controlling idea behind the poem in the pluralistic philosophy of William James who, in turn, is strongly influenced by Bergsonian duration: " 'Once adopt the movement of this life in any given instance and you know what Bergson calls the *devenir réel* by which the thing evolves and grows' " (p. 34).

[8] E.g., Altick and Loucks, in *Browning's Roman Murder Story*, say that the poem "lacks immediate conflict." The three protagonists "are limited to describing only past events as they remember them. The plot is mainly in the past, and the situations represented in the successive monologues are but the aftermaths of important events" (p. 8).

[9] See, e.g., Roy Gridley, "Browning's Two Guidos," *University of Toronto Quarterly*, XXXVII (October 1967), 51-68.

[10] B. R. McElderry, Jr., in "Narrative Structure of *The Ring and the Book*," *Washington State College Research Studies*, XI (1943), 193-233, presents tabular analyses which reveal the temporal ordering of all twelve monologues. McElderry points out that Guido's second monologue is a sharp structural contrast not only to Book V but to Book X as well: "To achieve this double contrast in the single book was perhaps one of Browning's most difficult structural problems" (p. 218).

[11] Concerning this line, Robert Langbaum writes, "A man who can say this about himself is not lost. Guido sees that since God made him, there must be a place in God's scheme even for him" ("Is Guido Saved? The Meaning of Browning's Conclusion to *The Ring and the Book*," *VP*, X [Winter, 1972], p. 295. Langbaum argues for Guido's salvation on the basis of self-illumination acquired in this monologue. I maintain that Guido's "insights" into himself are actually deceptions, or protective rationalizations, that further incriminate him.

[12] *The Poetry of Experience*, p. 111. For a review of the early critical controversy surrounding Guido's final utterance, see A. K. Cook, *A Commentary Upon Browning's "The Ring and the Book"* (New York: Oxford University Press, 1920), pp. 316-318.

[13] See, e.g., the otherwise thorough and illuminating analysis of Pompilia's language and character by Mary R. Sullivan in *Browning's Voices in "The Ring and the Book,"* pp. 86-100. More recently E. Warwick Slinn reinforces the view of Pompilia as a character who, unable to "adapt to the world's realities," handles the pain of her existence "by denying its substance" (*Browning and the Fictions of Identity*, p. 126). Viewing denial in a different light, Kay Austen, in "Pompilia: 'Saint and Martyr

Both' " (*VP*, 17 [1979], pp. 287-301), interprets Pompilia's dissociation from human life as evidence of her saintly perfection.

[14] I do not mean to overlook entirely a troublesome but frequently quoted comment Pompilia makes regarding her meeting with Caponsacchi: "no change / Here, though all else changed in the changing world!" (1401-02). Although the comment seems strikingly inappropriate, critics readily accommodate it to the familiar theme opposing earthly mutability to heavenly permanence. Altick and Loucks, for example, write: "Both Pompilia and Caponsacchi are, at the outset, victims of change and uncertainty. . . . Transformation to pure spirit that is forever impervious to change, says Browning, is the promise Christianity offers to those who would escape the flickering shadows of the mutable world of men" (*Browning's Roman Murder Story*, p. 111). A close reading of the monologues of Caponsacchi and Pompilia reveals, however, that far from being "victims of change" they are most threatened by its absence. Altick and Loucks, in fact, appear to change their own minds, for later they write: "Guido . . . boasts that he is 'changeless.' But to Browning the boast is, in fact, self-condemnation, for moral growth, which Guido renounces, is the very principle of human life" (p. 345).

The problematical nature of Pompilia's quotation is best addressed by one of two interpretations. First, Pompilia appears to use the word "change" here in the sense of deception, or discrepancy between appearance and reality, rather than temporal process. Only Caponsacchi proves superior to the deceit and treachery practiced by all others with whom Pompilia has had to deal. A second explanation is that Pompilia, far from directing resentment toward change as process, is marvelling over the experience of it. This interpretation, though it requires a shifting of emphasis, fits the context. Shortly before the troublesome passage, Pompilia describes her reaction to the knowledge of her pregnancy: "Up I sprang alive, / Light in me, light without me- everywhere / Change!" (1212-14). And shortly after, she announces that all new stars "grow [Caponsacchi]" who, as she discovers, makes "the shine everywhere" (1553-54). In the passage in question, then, Pompilia, newly awakened through change, expresses wonderment that only Caponsacchi does not change. The reason, she soon discovers, is that Caponsacchi represents the very force or principle of change itself — he is both the cause and the effect of change, and consequently he encompasses it all.

CONCLUSION

[1] See especially the exchange by Paul Cundiff, Robert Langbaum, and Donald Smalley, *VN* 15-17 (Spring 1959-Spring 1960), as well as Cundiff's attempt at a comprehensive last word on the subject in *Browning's Ring Metaphor and the Truth* (Metuchen, N.J.: The Scarecrow Press, 1972).

[2] *Matter and Memory*, trans. Nancy Paul and W. Scott Palmer (Garden City, N.Y.: Doubleday Anchor, 1959), p. 177.

³ John Macquarrie, *Twentieth Century Religious Thought* (New York: Harper and Row, 1963), pp. 27-28.

⁴ *Ibid.*, p. 237.

⁵ See, e.g., E. D. H. Johnson, "Robert Browning's Pluralistic Universe: A Reading of *The Ring and the Book*." Johnson compares Browning to William James and quotes James's defense of Browning and Whitman against the attacks of Santayana: " 'Give me Walt Whitman and Browning ten times over.... The barbarians are in the line of mental growth, and those who insist that the ideal and the real are dynamically continuous are those by whom the world is to be saved' " (p. 20). Admittedly, the alignment of Browning with the time philosophers is an annoyance to some. Thus, Wyndham Lewis, in his caustic polemic against the entire Bergsonian school, characterizes the attitude of the group with a sneering nod in Brown's direction: "Time being in its mercurial Heaven, all is well with the world of the little space-timeist..." *Time and Western Man* (Boston: Beacon Press, 1957), p. 153.

⁶ For the existentialist theory of perception see Thomas Hanna, *The Bergsonian Heritage* (New York: Columbia University Press, 1962), pp. 24 ff.

www.ingramcontent.com/pod-product-compliance
Lightning Source LLC
Chambersburg PA
CBHW061829040426
42447CB00012B/2887